W9-BST-133

It's a
mom
Thing

Jan King

STARK BOOKS

Andrews McMeel
Publishing

Kansas City

01 02 03 04 05 RDC 10 9 8 7 6 5 4 3 2

Library of Congress Catalog Card Number: 00-108495

ISBN: 0-7407-1407-4

Book design by Holly Camerlinck

With all my love to my mom and dad,
Betty and Frank Prahovic,
and to my late grandmothers,
Kathryn Beebe Gilbert and
Antonia Lugar Prahovic

Contents

CONTENTS

CONTENTS

Acknowledgments

To my publisher, Allan Stark, my eternal gratitude for your guidance and belief in me. You really understand what humor is all about, and bless you for giving me the forum to express mine.

To my editor, Kelly Gilbert—you're the bomb! There is no problem too large or small for you to solve. Thank you for your patience and your expertise, and for allowing me to stalk you on a daily basis with my obsessive-compulsive E-mails.

To the best P.R. gals on Earth, Monica White and Cyndy Purcell. You rock! Thank you so much for making miracles.

To my husband, Mark Chutick—what can I say but I love you and thank you till the end of time for being my strongest supporter.

To my sons, Michael and Philip—thank you for being the joys of my life. Also thanks for being so funny and providing me with lots of material. To Whitney, Sarah, and baby Joseph—you complete us all. Words can't express how blessed we are to have you as family.

Introduction

Okay. Listen up, ladies. *It's a Mom Thing* is required reading—that is, for anyone who can use some big laughs to get her through the day. And I'm just the gal who can provide them, because I am a mom and a stepmom besides being a humor writer. Come to think of it, I am also a wife. But I want to state categorically that I am not currently nor have I ever been married to either Alan, Don, or Larry King. At least, not that I can remember.

Being a mom isn't a piece of cake. God put us on the earth for one main purpose: to preach, teach, and nag, as Dr. Laura so aptly puts it. This is what we do best. We learned this from our own mothers plus from watching great role models like Mama Celeste, *I Remember Mama,* and Mama Cass. But now that the new millennium has dawned, there are forces afoot who are trying to replace us as authority figures. In the past, kids always went to Mom for all the answers. Now they go to mamma.com on the Internet for anything they want to know. It's no longer a case of "Mother knows best." Mamma.com knows everything.

Forget all those bogus sources. Go directly to *It's a Mom Thing* for the real scoop on what you'll need to know about being a mom in today's world. God knows, this mom thing requires the knowledge of Solomon, the patience of Job, and the wisdom of Alex Trebek.

Just the thought of becoming a mom is really intimidating to young gals. In fact, many of them are waiting longer and longer to have children. So if you're one of these women who have been putting off motherhood for so long that their breast milk is about to expire, take heart. *It's a Mom Thing* will answer every conceivable question you have about being a mom in today's world.

And when you've finished, if there are any questions you don't know the answers to, don't ask me. Call Regis for your lifeline.

Expectant Moms:

I Haven't Got Time for the Pain

Pregnancy in 2001 is a major deal. Expectant mothers learn everything they can about proper nutrition and the latest labor and delivery techniques, and they take intensive courses in infant care.

The good news is that young women today are taking their roles very seriously to ensure that their babies will be born in the best possible health. They are willing to change their diets and make all of the necessary sacrifices to achieve this goal. I take no issue with this. However, even though they may be incredibly well prepared today, the one thing my generation had over them was that even though we were pregnant, we still had *fun*.

I was of that generation whose motto was *"Piggis Extremis"*—loosely translated from the Latin to mean "Go ahead. Finish the Sara Lee cheesecake!" It was the best. To begin with, doctors didn't know jack about anything as compared to today. They let you do just about anything during your pregnancy short of bungee jumping off the George Washington Bridge.

Here's the deal. Back when I was in the hospital going through labor, they actually allowed you to smoke in the labor room! You heard me. Yeah, that's right. Lit up a tasty Marlboro right on the spot with my feet up in stirrups. Come to think of it—how appropriate. All I needed was the hunky guy from the magazine ad as my labor coach, and it would have been the answer to a preggo woman's prayers. And as soon as I was wheeled back to my room after an eight-hour, gut-wrenching delivery, what did I do? You got it. A post-delivery ciggie, baby. More satisfying than post-coital puffing any day of the week. Ride 'em, cowboy!

Oh, sure. I know that right about now all you tofu-eating, aerobicizing health nuts are sniffing extra oxygen from your portable canisters. You don't have to tell me. I've heard it all before. In fact, when my grown kids hear about my prenatal habits, they just about have a seizure.

My son always informs me that if I hadn't smoked all the way through my pregnancy and delivery, he would have been born with about 2 billion more brain cells. He could have been Einstein. All right, already. I have no excuse. My only defense is a good offense. I tell him: "Well, your grandmother smoked Camel unfiltered cigarettes when she was pregnant with me, so consider yourself lucky."

Also, the nutritional value of my "diet" during my pregnancy would've sent Dr. Spock hyperventilating into his baby booties. I chowed down on bologna sandwiches[1] and Wonder bread for most of my nine months of pregnancy. Plus, I drank tons of chromosome-busting diet colas and subsisted on a Big Mac for dinner. The doctors let you gain pretty much unlimited weight[2] and let you eat anything you wanted. When you had your regular prenatal checkup, as long as you were still breathing and had a heartbeat,[3] you passed with flying colors.

Another neat thing about the *"Piggis Extremis"* era was that they hadn't gotten around to putting those bummer warning labels about the dangers of fetal alcohol syndrome on liquor bottles. Thank God for small favors. There was nothing like getting a little schnockered on Saturday night to calm down a fetus who was doing a kickboxing demonstration on your uterine wall. After a couple of glasses of chardonnay, you were both in La-La Land. We're talking more passive than Gandhi.

What can I say? We thought of life as the Last Days of

---

1. Contained enough nitrates to preserve Lenin.
2. Up to the poundage of Ted Kennedy.
3. It only had to be the baby's.

Disco. Sure, we indulged ourselves. But we were happy and we delivered happy babies. At least, mine were happy until they became old enough to realize what I had been doing during my pregnancies. Excuse me—but I think nowadays we've gone a bit overboard.

Mothers are told they should breast-feed their babies for three to six months before starting them on solid food. They've got these "lactation specialists" who come to your hospital room and force you to produce more milk per day than a Norwegian dairy farm. And no matter how sore and cracked your poor boobs become, they still make you do it. I'll tell you one thing. If one of those La Leche women had decided to pay me a visit, she wouldn't have gotten past the armed guards I'd have posted outside the door. I would've had them whack her good with a giant can of Enfamil.

The amazing thing is that back in those days, doctors actually discouraged breast-feeding. They even gave you pills to dry up your milk. Pardon me—I mean terminate your lactation. Did I care? No way. Why? Did you ever see one of those nursing bras from hell? They were not only uglier but more complicated than the sanitary belt you had to wear after delivering. If I wanted to wear a bra that exposed my nipples, I'd have gone to Fredricks of Hollywood. I mean, just look at the size of those hooters on breast-feeding women. Give me a break. When they take off their bras, they must get whiplash.

As far as waiting three to six months to feed your baby

solids, thirty years ago this was considered a ridiculous idea. We moms learned very quickly that once you brought the baby home from the hospital,[4] the only way you were going to get a good night's sleep was to keep his tummy full. Every mother I know ran out and bought these ingenious gizmos called Infa-Feeders. They were like giant hypodermic needles you filled with milk and cereal. The babies sucked them dry in two seconds flat. Believe me, they were more satisfied than Pavarotti on pasta. They loved it. We loved it. They slept through the night. Everybody was happy. Postpartum depression was at an all-time low.

When your baby was a little older, but still couldn't hold the bottle by himself, we had another clever trick up our sleeves. We piled folded diapers and propped their bottles on them, so the bottle was always in direct contact with their lips. This freed us up to do other things, like lighting our Marlboro Lights.[5]

And as soon as the baby cut his first tooth, we'd throw him a piece of steak or whatever else was on our dinner plates. Made them happy as clams. You got a problem with that? We didn't have any "sissy" babies back then. Babies were real babies. As a result, you could stick our kids in just about any conceivable environment and they would thrive. Do you remember how many babies attended Woodstock? I rest my case.

---

4. We stayed for one month.
5. "Safer" levels of tar, nicotine, carbon monoxide, mustard gas.

What really blows my mind is to watch these six-month preggo women working out in my gym. These women are grunting and pushing so hard, you'd think they were in Lamaze class instead of an exercise class. It's a miracle that one of them hasn't actually delivered right there in class. All I know is that if their water breaks, my Air Nikes will have to double as flotation devices.

Don't you think that some gentle stretching exercises would be enough? My main concern is that if they keep doing stuff like those strenuous deep knee bends in their thongs, they might give themselves an episiotomy.

All I can tell you is that my prenatal workout consisted of pulling the pop-tops off diet colas. That was about the extent of it. However, the doctors did recommend doing Kegel exercises. They were supposed to make your labor and delivery go faster and smoother. But I was in such bad shape, first time I tried them, I sprained mine. But I persevered, practicing diligently every day. This was because I had only the best intentions for giving my baby a trauma-free delivery. Okay. That was 50 percent of it. The other 50 percent was that I was scared silly by having to go through the pain of labor and delivery.

So, I worked out like there was no tomorrow. In fact, after nine months I had strengthened my Kegel muscles to the point where I could bend down and pick up a tire. Look, Ma—no hands!

Preggo Mommio's Quiz

1. The most pain-free method of delivery in your mom's era was available by using:
   a. an epidural
   b. a saddle block
   c. twilight sleep
   d. napalm

2. When you were six weeks old, your mom took you right from the breast to:
   a. solid foods
   b. pureed fruits
   c. cereals
   d. TV dinners

3. Your mom's friends thought there was nothing wrong with providing you with plenty of:
   a. secondhand clothes
   b. secondhand cribs
   c. secondhand toys
   d. secondhand smoke

4. During an at-home delivery in your average com-
   mune, the umbilical cord was often tied with:
   a. a length of hemp
   b. surgical thread
   c. fishing line
   d. a roach clip

5. In your grandmother's day, there weren't any
   babies born out of wedlock because:
   a. of the strict moral code
   b. it disgraced the family
   c. there was no premarital sex
   d. the rumble seat was too small

6. Thirty years ago, the most common way to ease
   morning sickness was with:
   a. crushed soda crackers
   b. crumbled dry toast
   c. grated orange peel
   d. a rolled joint

7. In any era, the smartest way to breast-feed is by using:
   a. alternating breasts
   b. a breast pump
   c. nipple shields
   d. a wet nurse

8. For the well-being of the mother, doctors should always adhere strictly to the policy of:
   a. prescribing iron pills
   b. no flying after six months
   c. bed rest
   d. the two-drink minimum

The answer to all of the above is *d* as in *Darvon*.

  5–8 right: Doobie-doobie-do.
  1–4 right: No cigar.

CHAPTER
2

Mothers-in-Law:

Sleeping with the Enemy's Son

Mothers-in-law have, without a doubt, been given the worst press of all living species.[1] For me, the mere mention of the word *mother-in-law* conjures up the image of that creature who chased Sigourney Weaver around in her spaceship. Talk about dangerous liaisons. But I'm not the only one who feels this way. Mothers-in-law have always been a subject for controversy. Let's face facts. Everything about them is difficult. For openers, nobody ever pronounces their name correctly. Ninety-eight percent of the population incorrectly refers to them as "mother-in-law*s*." So right off the bat, this group spells nothing but trouble.

---

1. Including Whitney Houston.

Every time I hear the term *mother-in-law* it brings to mind the Coasters' hit of the '60s. It's one of those songs that stay in your head forever. Remember the lyrics? "The *worst* person I know (mother-in-law, mother-in-law). She worries me so (mother-in-law, mother-in-law). . . ." And so it goes.

In the words of the great humanitarian and philosopher Rodney Dangerfield, "They don't get no respect . . . no respect at all." The old joke goes that the punishment for bigamy is getting two mothers-in-law. There is a lot of truth in humor. Throughout the years, mothers-in-law have been blamed for everything from breaking up marriages to murder. Do they really deserve this rap? I guess it depends on who you're talking to. But if you're talking to me, I'll be happy to spill my guts.

I'm kind of an authority because, so far, I've had three of them.[2] Being totally honest, two out of the three were real sweethearts. But the one that wasn't made up for the other two—in spades, clubs, and diamonds. That one made Lucretia Borgia look like the Flying Nun. From the first moment I met her, I could tell she was trouble. I could also tell she was whacked out on medication.

My mother-in-law's name was Marabelle and she was (big surprise) born and raised in the Deep South. Well, shut my mouth.[3] She took pride in telling everyone that she was

---

2. If I tell people I'm seventy-five, it doesn't make me look as bad.
3. Words you never heard out of her.

descended from some kind of grand southern heritage. Marabelle always bragged about her family tree. The thing was, it didn't fork. Went straight up like a telephone pole. But that's another story. Although there were some things I did like about her, the two things I didn't like about her was her face. Talk about a backstabber. She could have given lessons to O.J.

Marabelle was one of those demented southern mothers right out of a Tennessee Williams play. She was a widow, living quite contentedly with her thirty-three-year-old son, when we got engaged. This is the part where you scratch your head and say to yourself, "What the hell was she thinking?" Okay, go ahead. I can take it. I'm wounded but still standing. The thing is that you always think that your situation is going to be different. I believed that one day, Marabelle would come to the realization that she wasn't losing a son but gaining a daughter. Wrong. She saw it as losing a son and gaining a migraine.

Marabelle felt that I was totally unsuitable for her son. She based her feelings on these three "character flaws":

1. I was a Yankee.
2. I was divorced.
3. I was Catholic.

How's that for being the triple crown of trailer trash? She made it clear from the very beginning that she thought I was beneath her son—and countless others.

Here's a profile of Marabelle, so you can get an idea of what she was all about.

NAME: Marabelle Jefferson Adams Beauregard Lee

AGE: Changes more often than the prime rate

RESIDENCE: Lives in the state of denial

POLITICAL PERSUASION: Somewhere to the right of Genghis Kahn

PERSONAL HEROES: George Wallace, James Earl Ray, and the captain of the *Amistad*

LIKES: Southern belle dresses covered with dust ruffles, big picture hats, and crisp, white sheets

DISLIKES: Any trash-talkin' Yankee who marries her son

HAIRDO: Has worn her hair in the same style since the Truman administration. It's the classic southern "big hair" coif, sometimes called "the helmet." Each individual hair shaft is teased and reteased until the split ends reach a volume equal to the Astrodome. Then it's sprayed with enough hair spray to immobilize a buffalo. The color of her hair is hard to describe. Let's just say that this shade hasn't existed since the Ford Fairlane was discontinued.

CULTURE: Marabelle thinks of herself as a very cultured woman. She does spend a lot of time in museums, I'll give her that. I know for a fact that she has walked straight past hundreds of old masters. Her idea of really fine art is anything on the walls at Graceland.

Okay, enough with the bio. Now I'm going to get to the

really creepy part. When I saw that movie *Hush,* starring Jessica Lange as the psycho, southern mother-in-law, it really shook me up. The plot was a little too real for my liking. All I have to say is, thank goodness my divorce was final before this film was released. I wouldn't want Marabelle to have gotten any crazy ideas from seeing it. As it was, she had plenty of her own.

Jessica Lange played Martha, the nut-job mother-in-law who was insanely jealous of her new daughter-in-law, Helen, played by Gwyneth Paltrow.[4] Martha was determined to break up her son and Helen. She tried to get rid of her by:

1. having her mugged
2. having mugged rats fall on top of her
3. putting poison in her sweet-potato pie

The first two attempts gave Helen a few bruises and a new fur coat. However, the sweet-potato pie nearly did her in. But not from the poison. The sugar content put her into a diabetic coma. But luckily, she survived. She also got pregnant. Go figure. That's what's known in the cinematic arts as a non sequitur.

The final straw came during Helen's labor. Martha helped deliver the baby, but only allowed Helen an extra-strength Tylenol for her labor pains.[5] That's when it finally dawned on Helen that her mother-in-law did not have "warm fuzzies" for

---

4. And her hair extensions.
5. And a bullet to bite on.

her. It also didn't help Helen's plight by being married to that dufus son, Jackson. What a wimp. The guy never had the guts to stand up to his mother. He was always conveniently "away" when Helen needed him. Jackson was just like a place mat—the only time he showed up was when there was food on the table.

But Helen had the last laugh—all the way to the bank. First, she thwarted Martha's attempted escape by simultaneously letting the air out of her tires and her hair. This left Martha with a very uncertain future—and feeling terribly deflated. Helen also fixed her wimpy husband's wagon. Then she made him sit in it and sign the plantation over to her. You go, girl! Don't you love happy endings?

I'm a mother-in-law myself, but I have a whole different take on the situation. When my son announced he was getting married, I did not burst into tears or threaten to O.D. on Premarin. No way. I'm a survivor who has raised two sons to adulthood. When they were kids, I lost my voice every morning yelling at the top of my lungs for them to get out of bed for school. When they were teenagers, I lost sleep staying up half the night, worrying until I heard the car pull into the garage.

Even now when they're all grown up, there's still plenty of times when they make me lose my temper and go ballistic. So I figure that by gaining a daughter-in-law, the only thing I'm losing is all those headaches. You think I'm going to sit there crying about it? Get real. I'm celebrating. I've paid my dues. This was my world and now she's more than welcome to it!

Top Ten Tip-offs Your Southern Mother-in-Law Is Trouble

1. Lowers the Confederate flag on the days you have sex with her son.
2. Thinks *Damnyankees* is one word.
3. Only person who was ever thrown out of the Museum of Tolerance.
4. Refers to the Pope as "Hizzoner."
5. Carries a carpetbag by Fendi.
6. Garnishes your juleps with Feen-a-Mint.
7. Calls her plantation "Bigotland."
8. Makes you eat dinner in the kitchen with the help.
9. Insists on wearing a black armband to your wedding.
10. Her portrait hanging over the mantel has "Exhibit A" written across it.

CHAPTER
3

Dr. Mom:

Physician, Heal Thyself

Many of today's moms have ambitions to be more than just stay-at-home caretakers. We can enter the male-dominated world and become physicians, attorneys, accountants, or even stockbrokers.[1] As the song says, "You've come a long way, bay-bee."

But there is one thing we still are not allowed to be—and that is *sick*. When you are responsible for getting your kids to their all-important activities like soccer practice, gymnastic events, and Scout meetings, you simply cannot afford to be ill. After all, these are events of global magnitude that

---

1. Can you spell *sexual harassment?*

take precedence over any of the documented diseases in *JAMA* you might happen to contract. Decapitation is not a valid excuse, either.

When you have kids, it's hard *not* to get what they're carrying. They are continually bringing home viruses far more destructive than the ones that crash millions of hard drives annually. Every day of the year, our kids infect us with new types of cold and flu bugs, intestinal viruses, and bacterial infections. In fact, we're exposed to more strains than "The Blue Danube." The thing is, though, when the kids get a bug, they are a little under the weather for about twenty-four hours. Then they bounce back faster than George Jones from a binge. But when we get one of these bugs, we're not only under the weather, we're stalled by a whole frontal system.

Unfortunately, our immune systems have been weakened over the years from bad habits like eating tuna containing more lead than number 2 pencils, drinking countless toxic diet colas, and dining on street-vendor cuisine. So when we get a bug, it's automatically ten times worse than when our kids get it. At least, it's that way for me. Most twenty-four-hour viruses that attack my puny body can live there comfortably for at least three weeks.

Here's a factoid for you: Laundry, carpools, dinners, and other domestic things wait for no one. How many times have you been in bed with a flu and 104-degree fever, so sick that you saw a bright light in a tunnel with your dead relatives waving at you? But are you allowed to go? No way. You have to drag yourself out of bed, throw sweats on over your pj's, and drive the kids to school.

I'll tell you what women need. We need medical clinics that have drive-through windows with doctors on call twenty-four hours a day. Then we could pull up, recite our symptoms into a huge clown head, and drive to the take-out window for our medication or flu shots.[2]

We moms should be awarded honorary medical degrees. After raising our kids to adulthood, we have learned to identify and treat every disease ever written up in the pediatric journals. We could make Dr. Spock look like a wet nurse.

Do you remember all the sleepless nights you spent administering Tylenol every two hours for your child's fever? Then when it soared up there to 104 degrees, you quickly plunged him into a tub of ice-cold water. We did this with all the skill of a pro, because we had practiced it thousands of times before when unmolding custard cups. Also, from years of experience, by merely laying a hand on our children's foreheads, we could tell their temperatures within a .0001 margin of error.

Dr. Mom also has to become an expert in the field of emergency medicine. By the time our kids are four years old,

---

2. Along with our Happy Meal.

we have honed our trauma skills to the point where we can give faster and better treatment than the entire triage unit of *ER*. Every time your kid goes out on his bike, the odds are that he's going to do "wheelies" at thirty miles per hour and wipe out on some gravel road somewhere. Then he shows up at your back door, bleeding profusely from the cuts and scrapes covering every part of his body that his Sears Tuffskins[3] aren't protecting. He's got blood pouring down his face from his scalp wounds, smeared all over his scraped arms, and seeping through the knee patches on his jeans.

So for the next hour, you are alternately applying iodine and picking the gravel out of his scrapes with a tweezer. All the while, he's screeching for you to stop, that you are "killing him." Oh boy. And how is your day going? So all the while you're thinking, "I'd like to put this kid under general anesthesia."

You can always count on the fact that when any of these catastrophes happen, your husband is never around. Or if he is, he stages a disappearing act more convincing than Salman Rushdie's. Even though men sit there and revel in the blood and gore of Mike Tyson chewing off another guy's ear, when their kid gets a little boo-boo, they can't take it.

Ditto when your kid is suffering from an intestinal flu and vomiting on cue every ten minutes. Your husband conveniently comes up with a project that "absolutely can't

---

3. Same material used in the Ringling Brothers big top.

wait"—like polishing his lug wrench or crawling under the porch looking for termites.

So you run to the medicine cabinet and pull out all the medications you need to get into your sick kid, *stat*. That's when you discover that no matter how many ways you line up the arrows on the lids or push down and twist on the childproof caps, those suckers just ain't gonna open. Nope. Meanwhile, from the ungodly sounds that are coming out of the bathroom, you can tell that your kid is going Round-Three with the diarrhea and vomiting.

In utter frustration, you begin to smash the plastic bottle against the wall, bruising three knuckles in the process. Damn! Where the hell is that husband of yours when you need him? Better yet, where is his lug wrench?

My kids grew up a lot more medically sophisticated than most because their dad is a doctor. We've all heard the stories about medical students developing psychosomatic symptoms of every disease they study.[4] Well, I've got news for you. So do their kids.

When my son was six years old and accidentally fell off his swing one day, he told me it was because he must have "low blood pressure." In the classic words of Dave Barry, "I am not making this up." Then, when he was ten years old, he

---

4. Their wives actually contract them, though.

had a bellyache and kept telling me it was appendicitis. But I held firm to my diagnosis that he must have eaten something that didn't agree with him. Well, sure enough, the next morning we took him to the hospital for an emergency appendectomy. Thanks for the hot tip, Quincy.

Of course, I have never heard the end of that one. It's been over fifteen years and my son delights in recounting the time he almost died from Mom's "misdiagnosis" and "medical ignorance." I'm surprised he hasn't hit me with a major malpractice suit. What nerve!

Well, I have something I want to say to him about that incident. In a word—*Ooops.* Okay, maybe I didn't take him seriously. I must have subconsciously been getting even with him for all the times I was sick and still had to chauffeur him around even though my fever was so high I was burning up faster than *The English Patient.*

And now that TV shows like *ER* and *Chicago Hope* are so popular, kids are more medically savvy than ever. Nowadays, self-diagnosis is a huge part of their maturation process. A simple bellyache can be diverticulitis, a headache could possibly be meningitis, or a fever and rash could herald an infection from deadly flesh-eating bacteria. These days, our kids know so many medical terms, they're able to come up with a medical condition that will get them excused from almost anything—gym class, a physics test, or their own weddings.

• • •

When I was a kid, we never had the resources for learning how to feign an illness with the total professionalism that our kids have. About the best we could do was stick a thermometer in hot water to produce a high temperature. But our kids have access to very sophisticated training films like *Ferris Bueller's Day Off*—this is considered the bible for learning how to fake an illness for ditching school.

Young people must admit, it's a whole new medical picture out there. And they can scan it[5] right off the 'Net. Need to make a cast for your "broken arm" to get out of an algebra test? Visit the "Scams R Us" Web site. How about a condition that will prevent you from going on that lame trip with your parents? Check out www.disease du jour.com. And when the stakes are really high, like for final exams, go to www.eeg.com to learn how to generate a pretty convincing flat line on your monitor.

Dr. Mom's Multiple Choice Medical Quiz

1. What is the first symptom of an intestinal flu?
   a. fever
   b. chills
   c. headache
   d. carpet stains

---

5. Or scam.

2. What is the most effective R_x for teething?
   a. a teaspoon of paregoric
   b. a tray of ice cubes
   c. an ounce of Ambesol
   d. a shot of Jack Daniels

3. What is the most common cause of stomachaches in children?
   a. constipation
   b. intestinal virus
   c. *E. coli*
   d. vending machine food

4. What is an adult's worst medical nightmare?
   a. heart attack
   b. stroke
   c. no insurance
   d. childproof cap on the Kaopectate bottle

5. What should be the number one qualification when choosing a pediatrician?
   a. must be board certified
   b. must be in a group practice
   c. must be hospital affiliated
   d. must be a ringer for George Clooney

6.   What is the best treatment for scratching and itching?
     a. hydrocortisone
     b. calamine lotion
     c. petroleum jelly
     d. flea and tick collar

7.   What is the most common surgery kids have by
     the time they reach puberty?
     a. tonsillectomy
     b. appendectomy
     c. bunionectomy
     d. rhinoplasty (nose job)

8.   What is the first thing you should look for when
     diagnosing a case of flesh-eating bacteria?
     a. raised red rash
     b. blood poisoning
     c. high fever
     d. missing limbs

9.   Which is the most common substance children
     O.D. on?
     a. aspirin
     b. Tylenol
     c. vitamins
     d. Hostess Twinkies

10. What's the most effective treatment for baby's colic?
    a. warm milk
    b. bananas
    c. paregoric
    d. earplugs

You got it! D was the correct answer to every question. Yes—*d* as in *duuuuh*.

8–10 right: honorary medical degree from Harvard.
4–7 right: honorary degree from U. of Puerto Vallarta.
0–3 right: honorary degree from Dr. Jack Kevorkian.

Sex Ed Moms:

Endangering Wildlife

Moms have more than their share of thankless jobs. Changing diapers, carpooling, and science projects rank up there with the worst. But the one that moms dread most of all is having to deliver the old "facts of life" speech to their kids.

Just the thought of doing it is scarier than seeing Newt Gingrich in a thong. Nobody wants to face it. In fact, "the talk" could clear a room faster than a Yoko Ono album. However, I must say that nowadays moms get a break because most of our job has been taken over by Showtime After Hours features. By the time your kid is six years old, via the magic of cable TV, he has a greater working knowledge of sex than you do.

Also, the good old U.S. government recently has been doing their fair share to loosen the chastity belts of America. When your kids are asking about sexual matters or techniques beyond your scope of knowledge, have them watch the six o'clock news for up-to-the minute coverage.

I remember back in the '50s when my mom sat me down to explain the process of menstruation. She delivered this symposium using the only resource book printed in those days, called *Growing Up and Liking It*. It was apparent to me, however, that she wasn't liking it one bit because she wore a paper bag on her head during the whole speech. You've got to remember that back then, everyone was so repressed, anything sexual was kept in the closet along with J. Edgar Hoover's lingerie.

When I was ten years old, I was totally clueless about my body. The only thing I knew about a period was that it belonged at the end of a sentence. So when my mom told me about the changes my body was going to go through every month, I said, "Boy, that stinks. I wish I had a penis." But on second thought, I was having enough trouble getting into my pants as it was.

The thing was that back in those days, everything was considered a taboo subject. And having your period was about the closest thing to a terminal disease you could get. Our moms took this "unnatural condition" very seriously and once a month they became Menstrual Nazis, enforcing this strict code of rules:

Mom's Rules for '50s-Period Etiquette

1. *Tampons were strictly taboo.*[1] We were forced to wear one of those stupid sanitary belts, which were so complicated it required an engineering degree from MIT to attach the pad correctly.

2. *Taking a bath was verboten*—only sponge baths were permitted. As a result, this pretty much eliminated our chances of being voted Most Popular Girl throughout our entire school career.

3. *Cramps had to be suffered without medication.* Rather than risking addiction to Midol, our mothers chose to send us to bed with a hot water bottle whose only therapeutic effect was to heat up the sheets.

4. *No physical activity during our "heavy days."* This was just as well, because we were rendered immobile from wearing those old-fashioned sanitary pads, which were as big as queen-size mattresses.

5. *We were instructed to say we were having "our friend."* The words *menstruation* and *period* were just too graphic for those days. What's more, the term *vagina*

---

1. Before Prince Charles expressed the desire to be one.

was never to be uttered by anybody under thirty-five years of age without a medical degree. If we had dared say that word in front of our moms, they would have become catatonic.[2]

Even the magazine ads back then couldn't show a picture of the actual sanitary pad or even describe what it was used for. They were only allowed to show pictures of the box with the cryptic words *Modess . . . because. . . .* printed on the ad. So all of us girls under twelve spent most of our prepubescent years trying to figure out just what the hell was in that box.[3] And when we got up the courage to come right out and ask our moms, "What is a sanitary napkin for, anyway?" they would get all flushed and always give the same answer: "It's a clean piece of linen for the dinner table, dear."

But today, they shove these pads in your face every two minutes on TV commercials. What's more, they're pouring blue fluid into them to demonstrate how much they can absorb. I'll tell you one thing. If my body was dumping that many cc's into a pad, I'd need a D&C.

In direct contrast to the '50s, today's girls never let their periods dictate what they wear or what activities they can do. They go to the gym, swim, and wear skirts short enough to

---

2. The *Vagina Chronicles* would have killed them.
3. And did it come with a prize—like Cracker Jack?

tell when they're ovulating. Nobody hides anything from any-body anymore. Millennium moms feel compelled to explain the function of every body part to their daughters when they are very young. They teach them to use all the correct anatomical terms, too. Nowadays, don't be surprised when you hear some five-year-old kid casually drop the word *vagina* or *penis* in a conversation[4] with her little pals.

An equally stressful duty for moms is tackling the "where do babies come from?" question. This was so embarrassing for my mom, she actually delivered it from behind a screen—just like the criminals on *America's Most Wanted*. She gave the speech without ever actually uttering the words, *penis, sperm, vagina,* or *orgasm*. What a coup!

She told me in very vague terms that when mommies and daddies were feeling "very close" and loving, they joined together and God gave them a baby. Since it seemed like my parents fought all the time, it made perfect sense that they only had two of us kids.

And if we came home and asked Mom what "it" meant when Katy said her parents "did it" every night, she always handled it in her own forthright and mature fashion: "I have no idea what she's talking about, dear. Now, go and wash your hands for supper."

In today's culture, we have built museums with giant

---

4. About birth-control methods.

replicas of our anatomical systems for the purposes of sex education. Third graders can be taken on a tour of the entire reproductive system, walking through giant fallopian tubes into the uterus.

Giant IMAX screens show sperm enlarged to the point where they look like the Loch Ness monster. The teacher explains how it takes millions of male sperm to fertilize an egg because they won't stop for instructions. Nowadays, nothing is too sensitive or too out of bounds to explain to our kids. By the time the kids leave the building, they have a knowledge of eggs, sperm, and the reproductive system equal to Masters and Johnson.[5]

In the year 2001, the biggest on-ramp to the sexual highway for kids is the Internet. They just log on to some Web site like www.embarrassingtopics.com and read about any sexual topic they want to learn about. In fact, these Web sites get more hits than one of Ike Turner's dates.

Ten Most Asked Sexual Q & A On-line

Q. How do you know when you need to use a feminine moisture replacement?

A. When you can't walk without sustaining friction burns.

---

5. Or David Crosby.

Q. How do you know when you have a yeast infection?

A. When you're sprouting muffins.

Q. Is the female condom very cumbersome?

A. Not if you insert it with a shoe tree.

Q. Is it true that pesticides are killing men's sperm?

A. Only if they spray Raid down their pants.

Q. Is sex with multiple partners dangerous?

A. Only if it's done simultaneously.

Q. Why did I fail my Pap test?

A. Did you study for it?

Q. Can an IUD be removed without a general anesthetic?

A. Only by using the Heimlich maneuver.

Q. If you lose your tampon string, are you still able to get the tampon out?

A. Not without a search party.

Q. After a hysterectomy, will I be filled with remorse?

A. No. You'll be filled with gas—and enough to launch the Goodyear blimp.

Q.   Will sex be the same after my hysterectomy?
A.   Yes, it will be every bit as boring as before.

Moms of today need a degree in epidemiology to educate their kids about the host of dangerous organisms they could acquire through unprotected sex. You have to know about herpes, AIDS, chlamydia, the papilloma virus, and hundreds more. It seems like about the only way to make sure that your kids are having safe sex is to boil their dates.

It's such a shame that because of all the promiscuity in our society, we are forced to provide this kind of information to our kids when they begin dating. It was so much easier in my day. The only kind of protection you took on a date was a gun.

Mom's Sex Ed Quiz

True or False
1.   A *ménage à trois* is a French restaurant.
2.   The medical literature reports that you can achieve the best orgasm of your life by using Clairol's Herbal Essence shampoo.
3.   A Victoria's Secret thong should be sold with a tube of Monistat.
4.   The acceptable sexual roles of the new millennium are: heterosexual, homosexual, and first available.

5. Viagra for women is ineffective because they will fake taking it.
6. *Coitus interruptus* is Latin for "I forgot my diaphragm."
7. Most women agree the safer and less painful alternative to a tubal ligation is vasectomy.
8. Prior to 1970, any baby born before nine months was called a "preemie."
9. Years ago, moms said it was a good thing to act like a Madonna.
10. A man will only grovel at your feet so he can look up your dress.

All of the above are true.
7–10 right: Good girl.
4–6 right: Bad girl.
1–3 right: Pregnant girl.

Hippie Moms:

The Grass Is Always Greener . . .

Picture this. It's the '60s. Guys and gals have tuned in, turned on, and dropped out. Young adults spend all their time at folk festivals, strumming guitars and singing along with Bob Dylan and Joan Baez.[1] Your friends are into dropping acid, doing 'ludes, and injesting whatever illegal substances they can score at love-ins. In fact, their apartments contain enough grass to resod Wimbledon.

So one night when you and your boyfriend are sharing a doobie and a barrel of Rocky Road, you have one of your "grounded"[2] conversations about the future. This is when you

---

1. Off key, of course.
2. While floating three feet above it.

come up with the idea that what you need to make your life complete is a baby. Brilliant! But what else would you expect from an era whose most intellectual achievement was *The Gong Show*?

This same scenario was repeated in millions of domiciles across America in those days—the end result being a generation of yuppies with names like Moonbeam, Sunshine, and Dweezil who are running corporate America today. The fact that these bright people were spawned from an era of drug-induced madness should certainly be considered another wonder of the world.[3] It's an even greater wonder that this generation was born with any brain cells left unfried considering the substances their mothers ingested while pregnant.

Even thirty years ago, women were enlightened as to the medical benefits of a few joints to curb morning sickness. Back then women were into raising not only their consciousness but a hell of a lot of cannabis as well. The "hippies" were pioneers in the philosophy of doing everything "naturally." It was de rigueur for a woman in that era to insist on enduring the pain of natural childbirth without anesthetics.[4]

Many became vegetarians and lived on communes, where they could raise their own crops organically. Their "love children" were brought up drinking wheat-grass juice

3. Along with Don King's hair.
4. First tangible proof that marijuana causes brain damage.

instead of Hi-C punch and snacked on alfalfa sprouts instead of candy.

But as with any standard bearers, there was a lot of hypocrisy going on in the cult. The adults kept a stash of munchies on hand for mass consumption during their compulsory pot-smoking binges. It was not unusual to find Good & Plenty, M&M's, popcorn balls, and Hostess Twinkies on the pantry shelves next to the sacks of whole-grain flour, oatmeal, and barley. *Bon appétit!*

Is it any wonder the kids raised in the midst of this alternative existence grew up with more issues than *Meet the Press*? Talk about pushing the envelope. These kids were brought up in atmospheres more extreme than George Carlin's monologues. During the week, they were home-schooled on communes and wore Birkenstocks instead of booties. On the weekends, they were driven in Volkswagen vans painted with wildflowers to places like Woodstock or as far off as Monterey.[5]

Here they were subjected to rock music at 3,000 decibels from amps the size of Mama Cass. At the same time they were getting their eardrums busted, their parents were also getting busted. But that's another story. The amazing thing was that these kids never complained about their lives. They were very passive children. You would be too, if you grew up breathing air that had enough grass in it to mellow out the entire country of Iraq.

---

5. Hippie motto: Have folk festival, will travel.

• • •

However, when this generation grew up, they were prime for initiating the world's biggest backlash against the whole hippie movement. As young adults, the first thing they insisted on was indoor plumbing. The second was a good haircut. Once they hit the college campuses, their days of being passive were over. They studied hard and became the world's biggest sharks, swimming in the same pool as all the other stockbrokers, lawyers, and insurance salesmen. Then they created a system of the most exploitative boiler rooms in the country, making millions of dollars in the process.

It should come as no shock that the children of hippie parents would all grow up to politically espouse any and all philosophies to the right of Charlton Heston. Remember, these were the same kids who grew up playing with their *Chicago Seven* dolls. They never knew that "the Weathermen" were people who actually predicted the weather. They grew up as a part of one ongoing protest movement. In later years, they fought back by supporting Nixon. It was a welcome change to the candidates their parents supported who got elected by siphoning off the votes from the mentally ill. Don't forget, these were the same folks who eventually were responsible for sending Sonny Bono to Congress.[6]

After having to watch their parents wear bad-looking tie-

---

6. And Cher to plastic surgeons.

dyed T-shirts and love beads for most of their teenage years, it was a logical progression for this generation to become infatuated with Brooks Brothers suits and Burberry trenchcoats. Who could blame them for turning to 100 percent cotton and silk after a lifetime of bulletproof polyester? One would be hard pressed to come up anybody who looked as bad as their parents wearing a Nehru jacket, except maybe, Milton Berle in drag.

Rebellious behavior is the hallmark of every generation. And the offspring of the flower children longed for one thing only—"normal parents." In fact, they were so desperate to have them, they carried pictures of Ozzie and Harriet around in their wallets. They grew up praying that one day they would come home to June Cleaver opening the door with a plate of home-baked cookies in her hand. Instead, what they got was Alice B. Toklas with a plate of her infamous brownies.

Hippie Moms' Quiz

1. What was the most popular form of exercise in the '60s?
    a. running a marathon
    b. skipping rope
    c. jumping on a trampoline
    d. rolling a joint

2. Who was chosen Miss America in 1965?
   a. Maryann Mobley
   b. Marilyn Van DeBur
   c. Donna Axum
   d. Janis Joplin

3. What was the most popular amusement back then?
   a. strumming the guitar
   b. singing folk songs
   c. tie-dying T-shirts
   d. ingesting funny mushrooms

4. Who was the most wanted criminal of the '60s?
   a. Lee Harvey Oswald
   b. Sam Shepard
   c. James Earl Jones
   d. Lenny Bruce

5. Which was the most popular family of that era?
   a. Cleaver family
   b. Nelson family
   c. Anderson family
   d. Manson family

6. What was the most popular appliance of the day?
    a. fondue pot
    b. Crock Pot
    c. steam iron
    d. roach clip

7. What was the '60s generation most known for spreading?
    a. nonviolent ideology
    b. theory of conscientious objection
    c. peace and love
    d. venereal diseases

8. What was the worst tragedy of that decade?
    a. JFK assassination
    b. RFK assassination
    c. Martin Luther King assassination
    d. the Kingston Trio

9. Most of the political ideologies of the '60s came from:
    a. the working class
    b. the Nixon administration
    c. Henry Kissinger
    d. *Laugh-In*

10. What '60s sex symbol bedded more men than any other?
    a. Marilyn Monroe
    b. Jayne Mansfield
    c. Ann-Margret
    d. Rock Hudson

The answer to all questions is *d* as in *Dig it!*
Peace and love, Jan.

Yuppie Moms:

Home, Home, on the Range Rover

I've never been a yuppie mom. I've never even played one on TV. But I've hung around so many of them throughout the years, I can give you a dead-on description of what makes them uniquely yuppie. They are a species of goal-oriented individuals who have planned their whole lives down to the minute in leather-bound calendars. Let's just say that they are more driven than Miss Daisy.

Besides raising kids, yuppie moms often have very impressive careers. They have studied hard in college to become successful professionals. In the process, they have developed an expertise concerning the ins and outs of the American educational system. This makes them especially fanatical about sending their kids to the best private schools money can buy. They want to make sure that their sons and daughters have a "leg up" for college.[1]

But the competitive urge in a yuppie mom surfaces long before the school issue emerges. During their pregnancies, they shop relentlessly to get the "right"[2] brands of baby furniture, infant wear, and bedding for the new baby. They think nothing of dropping a couple thousand bucks on the finest hand-crafted crib money can buy. Then they fill it with those exclusive Pratesi linen sheets. Nothing but the best for their kids to poop in and spit up on.

All baby clothes are purchased at full retail price from exclusive French boutiques. The only time you are ever going to see a yuppie mom in a thrift shop is when she's working her Junior League shift.

When it comes to buying baby shoes, it's the top of the line only. No Payless for them. They gladly pay more. The yuppie shoes of choice are Baby Stride-Rites at thirty-five dollars a pair—very pricey, considering the fact that the kids only get to walk around the house twice before their feet grow out of them.

Next challenge—toy procurement. Yuppie moms will kill to get their hands on the latest in toys, CD-ROMS, and chil-

---

1. Especially helpful for their daughters.
2. Approved by the D.A.R.

dren's videos for their little darlings. These moms would trek into places more dangerous than the Belgian Congo to bag that rare species, *Pat the Bunny*. They will even deal on the black market to get their hands on any available Tickle-Me Elmo if their kids cry loud enough. When Ty announced that it had decided not to make any new Beanie Babies, these same mothers went all the way to the Supreme Court to get an injunction against the company. They even picketed for the civil rights of the infamous Teletubbie Tinky Winky, when his sexuality came under vicious attack from Pat Robertson.

The quest for the "right" school starts early. It has become a common practice for yuppie moms to enroll their kids in the most elite private preschools during their pregnancies. They are literally peeing on the pregnancy stick in their left hand while filling out the preschool application with their right. We're only talking preschool here, but it's going to set them back about twelve thousand dollars per year. That's a lot of Crayola Crayons, baby.

It seems to me that yuppie moms take charge of running their daughters' lives a lot more than they do their sons'. This is because they have to make sure that their daughters are put in the proper environment, not only to achieve success, but more importantly to marry it. Once these daughters are matriculating, they need their mothers' guidance to steer them to the appropriate courses that best prepare them for a

life in upper-class society. Course selection becomes tanta-
mount to achieving this goal. Here's a typical course selection
for a girl in boarding school to help her successfully negoti-
ate yuppie adulthood:

Preppy Course Selection: Fall Semester

HISTORY: The History of Madras 101
HOME EC: Dim Sum Preparation 105
INDUSTRIAL ARTS: Mercedes Repair Shop 201
ECONOMICS: Portfolio Management
SEX ED: White House Internship Training

Besides all her other duties, the yuppie mom has to face more
than a decade of driving the kids back and forth to school and
related activities. Many of these prep schools are located in
very remote areas of Maine and Massachusetts, where cows
are counted in the local population. The moms will find that
they have put on more mileage in a year than Cher has during her entire career. But the yuppie code states that she can't
purchase just any plebeian SUV. She needs a car like a Beemer
or Range Rover that actually comes with a pedigree.

No flashy colors or big Caddies that look like pimpmo-
biles for yuppie moms. Anything with even a whiff of "nou-
veau riche" could be the deciding factor in getting
blackballed from the Junior League. The color also has to be

tasteful, like British racing green or Burberry tan. Likewise, the interior must be made of real leather and not some faux material like Naugahyde. Even the family rottweiler, Maximus Rex, wouldn't deign to pee on that cheesy stuff.

Once her kid is ensconced in the right school, the yuppie mom spends the next twelve years of her life engrossed in fund-raising activities. She is a tireless volunteer for school bazaars, fairs, and carnivals. The money raised for private schools goes toward providing educational necessities like a new chandelier for the dining room and sports bras.[3]

It's important for yuppie moms to involve themselves in making school policy. Many sit on committees that are very influential in deciding which extracurricular activities the school offers. They are crucial in helping the kids navigate their social responsibilities during school and after graduation. The following extracurricular activities are designed to help a young girl learn the social skills demanded of her:

Preppy Extracurricular Activities

1. Cotillion dancing
2. Dressage lessons
3. Sexual etiquette in the Ivy League

---

3. It's always important to support the student body.

4. Stalking boys with trust funds
5. Debutante ball hijinks

After the kids get out of high school, one of the most demanding phases of a mom's duties begins. It's preparing her children to confront their first life-and-death event—the SAT exam. To make it into an Ivy League college, the kids have got to perform exceedingly well on this test. The competition is fierce. In effect, their whole future depends on how well they score on this test. Especially because their uncle Evan got thrown out of Princeton eighteen years ago for Xeroxing his butt, which makes playing the legacy card impossible.

In bygone days, if your family had a blue-blood lineage, it would automatically get you entree into any fancy school. But in our present society, hardly anybody can trace their heritage directly back to the *Mayflower*.[4] Therefore, the elite schools have very strict policies about entrance requirements. They look for SAT scores well above 600 in math and English. So the parents make their kids take every crash course in SAT preparation they can find.

The yuppie mom dons her Banana Republic uniform and takes on the role of her life as a full-time drill sergeant, enforcing grueling study sessions. The kids literally become her prisoners of war, enduring weeks of solitary confinement

4. The ship—not the madam.

and withstanding punishments that would make John McCain look like a wuss. The good news is that even if these kids never get into college, they will be able to survive being captured by any hostile force on earth.

The Yuppie Mom Quiz

Here is an IQ test to see if you would make a good yuppie mom. Circle your response in the form of **A**lways, **S**ometimes, or **N**ever:

1. Have used influence peddling to get child into desired preschool. (A) (S) (N)

2. Have paid off proper people to obscure all family connections to rednecks. (A) (S) (N)

3. Have gone to court to have your names legally changed from Marge and Ralph to Bunny and Binky. (A) (S) (N)

4. Have paid up to $10,000 for a black market Cabbage Patch kid. (A) (S) (N)

5. Reject Pokémon for children on the grounds of racially mixed lineage. (A) (S) (N)

6. Are willing to pay $5,000 extra in tuition for your child to attend a school with the words *Country Day* in its name. (A) (S) (N)

7. Prohibit your children from ever taking a ride in a Winnebago. (A) (S) (N)

8. Would never entertain the idea of serving domestic champagne at your daughter's wedding. (A) (S) (N)

9. Would have no qualms about hocking the family burial plots to finance your daughter's debutante party. (A) (S) (N)

10. Frequently pepper your speech with phrases like "old sport," "gawd awful," and "top drawer." (A) (S) (N)

8–10 *A*'s: Congratulations, old sport. Welcome to the club.

5–7 *A*'s: You're on the waiting list.

0–4 *A*'s: Blackballed.

L.A. Moms:

Digging for Gold

Before I became an L.A. mom, I spent fifteen years on the East Coast raising my sons. Speaking as a bicoastal mother, I'd like to point out some of the cultural differences of each coast that affect how your kids are brought up. And because I am first and foremost a writer, you can count on a highly exaggerated and distorted version of what I experienced.

L.A. is a city that has righteously earned the name "La La Land." Everything that happens here is influenced by the movie industry. Fashion, education, lingo—whatever. All of it is dictated by what's currently going on in Hollywood. The scary thing is that this movie culture has a very profound influence in teaching morals to our kids. In my opinion, the kids out here grow up with very questionable values. Let's face it. When the biggest question on everyone's lips is "Who will father Madonna's next baby?" it's all downhill from there.

Thank goodness, the values are quite different on the East Coast. My kids were fortunate to have grown up in the small town of McLean, Virginia, population 150,000.[1] Because it's only a few miles out of Washington, D.C., it's a lot more intellectual in nature than the movie-crazed West Coast. In Virginia, we like to think that our moral code is far superior to La La Land's. Issues like the legitimacy of Madonna's babies are of no interest to us. We are much more interested in political issues— like the possibility of Clinton's illegitimate offspring.

Here's some of the main differences the moms of the East versus West Coast face when raising their kids:

FASHION ISSUES: I hang out with a lot of L.A. moms who are heavily into the "glamour" thing. Out here, women feel the need to compete with all the sexy, young movie stars. So they get totally sucked into the latest trends in exercise, diet, makeup, and provocative clothing. Cosmetic surgery is a necessity, not a luxury, in California. As a result, an L.A. PTA meeting looks more like a Hooters convention than a school event.

---

1. Ted Kennedy is counted as 30,000.

It's no wonder L.A. moms and their daughters have ongoing battles over their clothes and makeup. The normal issues that kids deal with growing up are made more difficult because these sexy moms are not the best role models for their daughters. Their own choice of clothing puts them in a "do as I say, not as I do" situation. The moms try desperately to dissuade their daughters from wearing inappropriate outfits like platform heels, skimpy tube tops, and skirts so short you can tell what day it is by their panties. And the same mothers who lecture their daughters about "suitable attire" for young ladies are wearing dresses that look like those worn by the night hostesses at Denny's. Go figure.

It takes two words to describe East Coast fashion—*the Gap*. All the gals wear those Laura Ashley dresses. You know the ones—those *Little House on the Prairie* dresses made to match their curtains and lamp shades. They're also into khaki pants and oversized sweaters the size of Rhode Island. East Coast girls have better coverage than Blue Cross.

Even at prom time, the moms don't have to worry about their daughters wearing cleavage-baring gowns or spike heels. These girls aren't trying to copy what Salma Hayek or Jennifer Lopez wore to the Grammys. Their idea of sex appeal is Jessica Fletcher at a Cabot Cove clambake.

EDUCATION: When my sons were students in Virginia, the curriculum was extremely tough. Michael, my oldest, went to a high school for kids gifted in science. Home of the brainiacs. The kids that went there made Stephen Hawking look like a first-round loser on *Who Wants to Be a Millionaire.* So when it came time for their yearly science projects, believe me when I tell you these kids came up with some doozies. One kid actually cloned a bunch of cheerleaders. Okay, I'm making that up. But trust me, they were probably capable of it.

In his sophomore year, Michael's project was building a laser with a power supply from a very intricate electronic board he wired. I'm still not sure exactly what its function was. But it was capable of detonating a nuclear bomb, that I'm sure of. This thing was so complex and state-of-the-art, he could have given lessons to Ted Kaczynski.

In contrast, I offer Exhibit F from the West Coast. Just last week, my girlfriend was bragging about the "science project" her kid was working on. I use the term in the loosest possible context, because after she described it, I felt it would better qualify as a home economics demonstration. Anyway, her son had to compare different brands of microwave popcorn, counting the number of kernels that popped in various timed intervals. Now I ask you—what on earth is a kid going to learn from this experiment other than the fact that Orville Redenbacher wears goofy-looking bow ties?[2] I rest my case.

TERM PAPERS: My younger son, Philip, went to Langley High School in Virginia for two years before we moved to California. Langley is an excellent public school, famous for these three things:

1. its innovative curriculum
2. its location—half a mile from the CIA
3. its life-size statue of Rush Limbaugh[3]

My son took this wonderful course called the History of Civilization, which combined history and literature. His term paper was about the influence Plato had on the political structure of the day. He did all his research at the Library of Congress and the piece was really impressive.

When we moved to California, I enrolled him in a private school, thinking that it might be more immune to the Hollywood hoopla than a public school. Wrong. When term papers were due in his literature course, these were some of the topics actually accepted: history of the Oscars, the Mariah Carey story, and the social significance of the *Rocky* series. Talk about tabloid journalism. This was apparently the training ground. If this stuff qualifies

---

2. Possibly admission to the Orville Redenbacher Institute for Popping Sciences.
3. In a Speedo.

as "educational," what the heck is considered entertainment? No wonder *Clueless* was such a megahit out here. It should have been released as a documentary.

HOLIDAYS: We moved to Iowa when our boys were still little guys, like five and seven years old. Let me give you a factoid about Iowa. It is not a state for sissies. You have to be superfit just to withstand the climate.[4] Winter began as early as October and it often snowed well into April. But March was the real killer.[5] In March, we'd have these blizzards that ripped through the state, dumping thirty inches of snow in twenty-four hours. My kids would have to waddle off to school with snow up to their little tushies in subzero temperatures.

You've got to understand that in Iowa, they *never* call school off on account of the weather. Blizzards, F5 tornados, drought, or flood—it's all just another midwestern day out there. The only time they would cancel school was for a cultural event of the highest priority—like a tractor pull.

On the other hand, people in L.A. are total wusses when it comes to the elements. That's because they don't have the foggiest idea of what the elements are. They think they are things like oxygen and carbon. Now, don't

---

4. Not to mention mad cow disease.
5. Somebody needs to inform O.J.

misunderstand. I'm not complaining. A year filled with gorgeous, sunny days suits me just fine.

But the thing is that because it rarely rains, when it does, the population goes bonkers. The city literally shuts down. This past year, we had three consecutive days of showers and the TV was shrieking with "Stormwatch 2000" warnings. Panic was rampant. There was a run on all the grocery stores.[6] People were cautioned to stay off the highways. The Starbucks clientele became narcoleptic. Some schools actually closed. This is one state that could stand a reality check.

The truth is that L.A. schools do close at the drop of a hat. Even their holidays are different from the rest of the country's. L.A. kids not only get all the presidents' birthdays off, but they also get Jimmy Stewart's, Bette Davis's, and Joan Collins's.[7] All I have to say is that when Bob Hope finally goes, they'll probably close the schools for a month.

MOM'S DUTIES: My duties as an East Coast mom were pretty simple. Every day after school, I'd chauffeur the kids to soccer, baseball, swimming, or tennis practice. My official mom's uniform consisted of an Old Navy sweatshirt, a pair of jeans, and a pair of beat-up tennies. East Coast

---

6. Brie and Evian were the first things off the shelves.
7. According to the Rosetta Stone, she'll be 106 next year.

moms don't feel they need to look glamorous. But what we need is patience. Heaps of it. Life as we knew it was all about waiting. Waiting in the bleachers for practice to end, waiting in our cars for school to let out, and waiting for our kids to grow up so we could have a life.

L.A. kids have an entirely different agenda. Their moms are also chauffeurs, but they drive their kids to auditions and casting calls. Instead of playing soccer, these kids would rather play the role of Pele in some local theatrical production. To L.A. kids, all the world's a stage and they are merely players.[8]

The moms doll up too, hoping they might get "discovered" at their kids' auditions, and land a supporting role where they actually get paid to play a mother. So when the kids become wildly successful and have their own agents, their people will call her people and arrange a family dinner.

PEER GROUPS: L.A. moms have a definite home-court advantage in helping to provide a suitable peer group for their kids. Because divorce is epidemic in California, many kids get the bonus of having extended stepfamilies. After multiple divorces, they may extend all the way to New Jersey.

But it's actually the divorced dads who provide the

8. With a SAG card and an agent.

greatest service in this area. This is because so many of them remarry gals who are little more than teenagers themselves. So weekend visitations with the kids turn into one big slumber party with ready-made girlfriends. However, it's the young wives who have the best of both worlds. Even if they get ditched in a couple of years, they're still so young they'll also be awarded child support besides their alimony.

Many East Coast moms don't have to shoulder the responsibility of finding suitable peer groups. This is because at the mere hint of a behavioral problem, East Coast parents all have the same solution—boarding school. For big bucks, their kids get to live in an environment with more rules than the Cider House. And if the kids are still hanging out with "undesirables," their moms issue this ultimatum: Shape up or ship out—to military school. Here, their new peer group will be composed of drill sergeants whose idea of a wild weekend is to make them hang out in the latrines, scrubbing toilets.

Top Ten Facts About L.A.

1. It's the only city where hairdressers earn more than heart surgeons.
2. Most showbiz careers are shorter than Mini-Me.

3. L.A. gangs are actually a socially conscious group—they're the only people out here that drive with more than one person in a car.

4. Cell phones are mandated by law.

5. It's the gold-digging capital of the universe as evidenced by shows like *So You Want to Marry a Millionaire.*

6. Stars like Robert Downey Jr. and Charlie Sheen are considered role models.

7. Dogs in Beverly Hills get their teeth capped.

8. The women in L.A. have had their faces pulled up more times than Ted Kennedy's pants.

9. L.A. cosmetic surgeons are groundbreakers in innovative techniques. The latest is abandoning the controversial silicone breast implants in favor of helium.

10. Besides the world-famous chain of Comedy Traffic Schools, L.A. has recently added the Halle Berry Driving Schools.

Jewish Moms:

Guilty as Charged

Jewish moms aren't all that different from other moms. Every mother loves to send her kids on guilt trips. But Jewish mothers are so good at it, their kids collect frequent flyer miles. The Catholic kids are lucky. They're able to get rid of their guilt in confession, whereas the Jewish kids schlep it around for life.[1] Another difference in a Jewish mother is the unique way she shows love to her kids. She does this by never missing an opportunity to tell them how much she has sacrificed for them.

Next to Joan of Arc and Gandhi, the Jewish mother ranks right up there with the world's greatest martyrs. The following

---

1. In humongous guilt bags.

are some of the statements their kids will hear on a daily basis for the rest of their lives:

1. "Do you know how much I suffered giving birth to you?"
2. "Who am I, Rockefeller?"
3. "Sure, put another knife in my heart."
4. "So, this is how you thank me?"
5. "Are you trying to give me a heart attack?"

We all agree that Mother knows best. But a Jewish mother knows better. This is because she wrote the book on worrying. She even has back-up worries besides her regular worries. Jewish moms view everything in the world as a source of potential danger. To counteract their fears, they issue more warnings than the Coast Guard during a nor'easter.

Here are just a few of the warnings their kids have grown up hearing:

1. "That will teach you to listen to your mother."
2. "Just wait till your father comes home."
3. "If you don't stop crying, I'll really give you something to cry about."
4. "Don't eat that—you'll ruin your appetite."
5. "Take a little sweater. You'll catch your death."

A Jewish mother is so fearful that some harm will befall her kids, she has to know everything they're doing at all times. This is why they have become notorious for nosing into their kids' lives.

Jewish moms don't know the meaning of the word *privacy*. In fact, they mind their own business less than Ann and Abby. She regularly ransacks her kids' rooms, snooping through her daughter's diary and confiscating her son's stash of *Playboys*. And God forbid she finds a condom, they'll have to call the paramedics. A Jewish mother calls this a routine room inspection. She studied surveillance at Quantico.

They are also experts at following their kids around trying to see what they're up to. This is why most Jewish kids have learned to travel under assumed names. Why are Jewish moms so suspicious? Well, to begin with, it isn't their fault. They're programmed to believe trouble is lurking around every corner.

A Jewish mom starts worrying the day you are born. When you're in the crib, she runs into the room every five minutes to see if you're still breathing. When you're ten, she runs in to see if you're studying. At sixteen, she runs in to see if you're having sex.[2]

The Jewish mother is reluctant to let her kids out of her sight for even a minute. The kids are in for one big fight if they ever ask to go far from home. Even if she says yes, they aren't going to get very far being attached to her apron strings. During their summer vacations, the kids have to beg her to let them go to camp. She has a horror of places like

2. Alone or with somebody else.

this. She firmly believes that if she lets her kids go, they'll end up drowning there.[3]

Jewish moms are sighted hovering more often than UFOs. They worry that their kids are going to get into all kinds of trouble unless they're around to supervise. This woe and misery the Jewish mom expects to come her way is called *tsuris* in Yiddish. After the kids come, she expects to suffer with it for a lifetime. A Jewish mother's best revenge is to live long enough to give it back to her kids.

Extracting information from her kids is a big part of a Jewish mother's agenda. She thinks this knowledge is going to make her worry less, but the more she knows, the more she worries. She has no conscience about how she gets her information, either. Jewish moms have been known to put surveillance cameras in the kids' rooms. And when this lady interrogates, she becomes more ruthless than Andy Sipowicz.

Jewish moms are world-famous for their frequent use of the rhetorical question. This makes them experts in asking, never answering. Having to answer to anything or anybody is not in their job description. It bugs them. They always have to keep total control in any conversation with their kids.[4] However, Jewish kids also have become pretty adept at verbally sparring back at her:

---

3. Most likely in the bathtub.
4. And a blinding spotlight over their heads.

MOM: "So, what about this girl you're dating?"
SON: "So, what about her?"
MOM: "Is she Jewish?"
SON: "Is the pope Catholic?"
MOM: "Listen, Mr. Smarty Pants, what do her parents do?"
SON: "You're asking if they have money?"
MOM: "Is this what I raised you for? To be a smart mouth?"
SON: "So, I shouldn't talk anymore?"
MOM: "Oy vey."

Besides being an expert private detective and champion guilt tripper, the multitalented Jewish mom also excels in another field—medicine. All doctors should do their training with Jewish mothers. Spock, shmock. She wrote the book. It's a well-known fact that the Jewish mom takes her kids' temperatures twice a day, whether they need it or not.[5] No matter how virulent the strain of flu, she's got one antidote—chicken soup. It's the Jewish penicillin. The kids learn so well from her that when they're finished playing doctor, they send you a bill.

Since a Jewish mother doesn't have her own medical license, she painstakingly searches for a doctor to treat her family. The standards this doctor has to meet are pretty impossible—but, then again, the guy is pretty impossible in his own right:

---

5. Resulting in twenty years of intense psychotherapy.

- *Must be socially prominent*—He must appear regularly in the social columns, photographed at important[6] charity balls.

- *Must have no bedside manner*—He is condescending and talks down to you, like you're someone's inbred cousin.

- *Must be impossible to reach*—You must book six months ahead for an appointment and be recommended by some highly placed person.

- *Must be in total demand*—Keeps you waiting in the reception area for the better part of Shabat.

- *Must be a ruthless businessman*—Sends a guy named Hymie the Hip to your home to collect on his astronomical bill if it's not paid within twenty-four hours of your visit.

Any professional is always held in high regard by a Jewish mother. This is her dream for her sons. But she thinks differently about her daughter. It's not important that her daughter become a professional herself, only that she marry one.

From birth, the Jewish mom begins the search for a professional man for her daughter to marry. Her preference is for a doctor, of course.[7] She becomes so expert in the art of matchmaking, she could put Tevye out of work. Over the course of

---

6. Minimum of a thousand dollars per plate.
7. And not one of those nebbish PhD's, either.

her young adulthood, the poor daughter will have countless blind dates. You can always spot a Jewish girl on a blind date her mother has arranged. She's the one wearing the wedding gown.

When the wedding day finally arrives, the Jewish mom will spare no expense. Outrageous expenses are a normal part of the Jewish tradition when marrying off their daughters. And to think that it all started from a fiddler on the roof.

Besides all the normal expenses, the Jewish wedding also boasts the following basics, putting the dollar amount just short of the GNP:

1. *The traditional tent*—made of white silk with a chuppa covered in orchids FedExed from Fiji.
2. *A calligrapher*—who charges $2.50 per curlicued letter to pen everything from the invitations to the place cards.
3. *A Viennese table*—featuring enough sugary desserts to require insulin shots for all the guests.
4. *A guest list of thousands*—including the Jewish mom's hair colorist, cleaning lady (seated at a table of honor), decorator, manicurist, and her entire mah-jongg group.[8]
5. *Ten Jewish cardiologists on call*—to provide emergency treatment for most of the guests who flew in from Miami.

---

8. The only things sharper than their acrylic nails are their tongues.

6. *The wedding album*—five thousand dollars for state-of-the-art digital photos of the guests who are out of focus from being loaded to the gills.
7. *The centerpieces*—have to be fashioned from six-foot-tall bird of paradise plants with four-foot-wide fronds in order to obscure the view between hated relatives on opposite sides of the table.

Jewish Mother's Dictionary

DELICATESSEN: A restaurant that serves six-foot-high sandwiches that cost thirty dollars.

FERCOCKTA: Woody Allen and Soon-Yi.

GOYIM NAKHES: A new motor home.

HAYMISH: Ron Howard.

LOEHMANNS: a.k.a. Cellulite City.

LOX: Jewish sushi.

MATZOH: Bread that looks like it needs Viagra.

MAZEL TOV: When the daughter marries a Jewish doctor or lawyer who isn't divorced twice already.

MEZUZAH: Sign on the door indicating the occupants don't go duck hunting.

MIESKEIT: Phyllis Diller.

SCHLEP: To travel without a limo.

SCHMUCK: Anyone who pays retail.

SHAEGETZ: Rick Rockwell.

SHANDA: When your daughter marries an Arab.

SHIKSA: Cause of a massive coronary.

SHTARKER: A guy who wears a wool suit without underwear (Lenny Bruce).

SEDER: Motivation to attend Jenny Craig.

TSURIS: Your son enrolling in auto mechanic school.

UNGEPACHKIT: Almost any hotel room in Miami Beach.

Christmas Moms:

The Worst Noël

Our families have come to accept the fact that most of us moms get pretty psychotic around Christmas time. Hey, it's not our fault. From the time we were little girls, we've been brainwashed into the fairy tale thing about having the "perfect" Christmas.

For years, we've been hooked on the pictures in subversive literature like *Better Homes and Gardens* and *Ladies' Home Journal*. After thoroughly studying those pictures, we get obsessed trying to re-create them in our own homes. We try to turn their staged fantasy into our reality. Right. The Unabomber has a better grip on reality. Our quest for that impossible dream is driving everyone around us to seek solace in the spiked eggnog.

Our M.O. starts as early as June, when we buy up all the holiday craft magazines we can find. They give directions, step by step, on how to create the perfect ornaments, table centerpieces, wreaths, and tree skirts. We become like pack rats, hoarding piles of ribbon, glue, Styrofoam, and every artificial pine branch made in Taiwan.

Then we spend hours making something out of nothing. Granted, the kids are starving and will be totally neglected for the next few months, but we are creating holiday magic! We can take a pine cone, glue on colored beads, and voilà! A festive tabletop Christmas tree. Toilet-paper rolls can be spray-painted and fashioned into candlesticks.[1] Lacy paper doilies and pipe cleaners make wonderful angels. And if we run out of ideas, we can always get a fresh supply from that arts and crafts Nazi, Martha Stewart.

We need a lot of space for all our stuff. So we commandeer our husbands' studies and turn them into our craft "intelligence centers."[2] Nobody but nobody is allowed into our rooms. Especially not the kids. We guard our stash more closely than a Colombian drug lord. For the next few months we're pasting, cutting, and sewing like an elf on speed.[3] We become crazed, but we can't quit. We have more invested in these projects than our IRAs.

---

1. We'll steal anything out from under you.

2. An oxymoron.

3. Red Devils is their drug of choice.

By the week before Christmas we have run ourselves ragged. It takes every last bit of our strength to write out all the Christmas cards and mail them. The kids instinctively know they had better keep their distance. Thank God for child labor laws, because if we could get away with it, we'd have them working harder than in one of Kathie Lee's sweat shops. One would be correct in saying we have definitely gone postal. But we cling to the motto of the seriously deranged: We will have a perfect Christmas even if it kills us.

When Christmas Eve finally rolls around, we have greater expectations than Dickens. Everything seems perfect. The house is more decorated than Colin Powell. Chestnuts are roasting on an open fire. We sit back in our Barcaloungers decorated with red velvet bows and dream of what lies ahead:

The Dream

A fire blazes and there is an ever-so-slight dusting of snowflakes on the windowpanes. You are beautifully dressed in your red satin blouse and frilly hostess apron, handing out eggnog to friends and family. There is a profusion of blooming red poinsettias everywhere you look. Tiny white lights twinkle from under lush pine garlands, and every hall is decked with boughs of holly. Fa-la-la-la-la.

The dream continues...

Christmas morning you awaken early, get the fire blazing, don your best silk robe and slippers[4] and tie your hair up with a lovely bow. Likewise, your husband dresses in his silk smoking jacket and matching ascot.[5] You creep into the children's room and gently wake them. Then you all proceed into the parlor, where your decorator tree and all the decorator-wrapped gifts will take their breath away. The children each take their proper place around the silk brocade tree skirt, opening their gifts. Then they take turns holding them up to show the rest of the family, commenting about how grateful they are for such blessed abundance.

After unwrapping the gifts, you serve a scrumptious brunch of croissants, jam, and hot chocolate. While the children are playing with their new toys, you will be happily preparing the Christmas dinner. This is served in the dining room, using your best china, crystal, and linens.

A regular scene from Currier and Ives . . . the perfect Christmas . . . a dream come true. Time to wake up, Mrs. Santa Claus! Like any of this is really going to happen. You'd have to be suffering a psychotic episode first.

I hate to be the one to burst your bubble, but after pur-

---

4. Could be called "gay apparel."
5. Definitely gay apparel.

suing this stupid Christmas dream for over thirty years and failing miserably every year, I gave up. Read on to see what *really happens* in homes all over America.

The Nightmare

Christmas Eve day is a study in what nightmares are made of. The kids are on dangerous sugar highs after stuffing their pie holes for seventy-two hours, nonstop, with cookies and candy canes. They're calling each other names like "poo-poo head" and "booger nose." So much for goodwill to men. You are ready to smack them silly when you stop and think: "No—no—this is all wrong. I should be decking the halls, not the kids."

Instead, your main function for the entire day will be to try to keep the kids from killing each other. There will be more small wars breaking out per minute than in Israel. The kids will arm themselves with paintball guns and annihilate each other. Goodwill to men.

By the time you get the kids into bed, you'll call the pharmacy begging them to refill your Valium prescription. After self-medicating, you're ready to tackle the job of setting out the gifts. There is no rest for the weary. Your watch says it's three A.M. And speaking of watch, you have been watching your husband attempt to put the jungle gym together for three and a half hours. By now, you seriously consider taking the freakin' screwdriver out of his inept hands and stabbing him with it.

He refuses to read the instruction manual.[6] So you are forced to do it; but it's written in Japanese. Even the illustrations go from right to left. You can't find part C, which is supposed to fit snugly into part A. What's more, you can't find any of the crucial brackets, nuts, or bolts because some nitwit at the factory forgot to put them in the box.

The next project is the bicycles. Of course, the tires are flat and the chains are off the sprockets—what else did you expect? Your husband looks at you and says, "Duuuh." This is a husband's way of saying you are expected to do everything from bicycle repair to constructing a chemistry lab. So just who the hell does he think you are—MacGyver?

When you fall into bed at five A.M., you are sweaty and smelly, and you have bicycle chain grease all over your silk blouse. Your dreams contain visions of vampire sugar plums sucking the life out of you. Thirty minutes later, you're awakened to the forty-eight-decibel shrieking of your kids, who are already fighting over who gets what.

The kids are literally bouncing off the walls, launching themselves off the jungle gym like human cannon balls. They are tearing into their gifts at warp speed. Talk about greed.

---

6. He's a man, isn't he?

Gordon Gecko has nothing on them. But they do stop to say "thank you" in their own special way:

"Hey, Mom. How come that creep Billy got Rollerblades and I only got a bat?"

"Mom, look at what that cheapskate Aunt Alice gave me—a lousy ballpoint pen!"

Naturally, your thoughtful husband is videotaping the whole mise-en-scène. You look like hell. You are wearing baggy sweatpants and no makeup. Your only consolation is that everybody loves you even if the camera doesn't.

The kids are caught in the act of being themselves— ghouls. The house looks like it was just hit by a 7.2 quake. *This* is your historical record for the family archives. You try to figure out what went wrong. What happened to the silk robe and smell of roasting chestnuts by the fire?

Before you can get the Pop-Tarts out of the toaster, the kids are out doing wheelies and other death-defying tricks on their new bikes. By now, you must know where this story is going to end up. You got it—in the ER, where some pimply-faced intern has to stitch up a bloody scalp wound and set a fractured collarbone. Welcome back to the land of reality. 'Tis the season to be jolly.

The Common Sense Christmas Quiz

1. Where is the most ideal place to spend the Christmas holidays?
   a. in Aspen
   b. in the Caribbean
   c. in New York City
   d. in a coma

2. Which Christmas tradition works magic on the senses?
   a. the smell of fresh pine needles
   b. the taste of eggnog swirled on the palate
   c. Jack Frost nipping at your nose
   d. a nip of Jack Daniels at your lips

3. Who would be the best person(s) to pay a visit to your kids on Christmas Eve?
   a. Santa Claus
   b. their grandparents
   c. the carolers
   d. an exorcist

4. When shopping at Toys R Us, try to keep your cost within:
   a. your credit card limit
   b. your holiday budget
   c. your weekly income
   d. your life savings

5. During the holidays, which one is a better alternative to eggnog?
   a. hot buttered rum
   b. cranberry punch
   c. hot spiced cider
   d. hemlock smoothie

6. Who is the best person for moms to consult before planning next year's Christmas?
   a. a professional party planner
   b. a caterer
   c. a loan officer
   d. Dr. Kevorkian

Merry Christmas to all
And to all a good night.
If you picked *d*,
You got them all right!

Partying Moms:

Excedrin Moments

The saccharine "Times of Your Life" commercial is cleverly written to evoke all kinds of warm fuzzies in moms. They stage these fam-fest scenarios like graduation with joyous relatives, moms and babies laughing in the rain, and grandparents hugging grandkids under the Christmas tree. Give me a break. Talk about in your face. This isn't the reality I know. The truth is that these scenarios account for only about .01 percent of real-life stuff.

You know what I remember as the "times of my life"? All those experiences when my nerves were strung tighter than Yo-Yo Ma's cello and I got headaches severe enough to require narcotics. But take heed. In real life, the events that cause this reaction come disguised in the slogan "fun for the whole family." Uh-oh. Whenever you hear these words, run for the hills and hide out in the first cabin you see.[1] To spare your sanity, here are just a few of these "must do" events that should be red flagged as "must miss":

Birthday Parties at Chuck E. Cheese

For three- to ten-year-olds, they feature screeching kids, blaring video games, and enough greasy french fries on the floor to warrant three lawsuits. The kids who were invited have spent the day getting hyped up on Mars bars. Their parents pull into the parking lot in huge SUVs stuffed to capacity with these obnoxious little darlings. They barely slow down to a stop before throwing the kids out of the car, directly into your face.

The entire three and a half hour Chuck E. Cheese birthday party experience is carried on at a decibel level capable of vaporizing your eardrums. It's your sole responsibility to keep your eye on thirty kids who are elbowing each other to get at the video games, throwing food on the floor, and running to the bathrooms every two minutes. By three P.M., as you're wrangling the last kid out of the bathroom, you have ceased to worry about the few perverts who might be hang-

---

1. Try writing manifestos while you're there.

ing out in there. All bets are off. As far as you're concerned, it's open season.

After gulping down four extra-strength Excedrins with your rum-and-Sprite Big Gulp, you turn your attention to the "goody bags." These are filled with dozens of little plastic trinkets manufactured in Taiwan with a fair market value of about .0002 cents. But for some arcane reason, getting the "goody bag" is a life-or-death proposition to these kids who all own three-thousand-dollar state-of-the-art iMacs. They will trample each other like weeds trying to be the first to grab their bag out of your hands. Then they will promptly dump the contents all over the table, and take off for the jungle gym.

The S.O.P. for all the parents is to arrive at least thirty minutes late for pick up. After taking one look at you, they'll offer to drive you to the nearest ER. They know from their own experience that it would have been less stressful for you to have spent the afternoon getting hijacked in a 747.[2]

Family Ski Trips

In our society with its screwed-up values, parents consider themselves failures if they don't have their kids skiing before they're out of diapers. I don't know why we come up with these wacko ideas, but trust me, they're out there. I admit succumbing

---

2. Or landing it solo at O'Hare.

to the enormous pressure of this yuppie standard early on. We even traveled to Colorado for vacations, just so our kids would learn how to ski really well. They had friends who already were so skilled at this sport, they were skiing black slopes in the treacherous back bowls at Vail.

Skiing is not my idea of a great vacation. My preference is to park my butt on a lounge chair in Hawaii for a week and move as little as possible. A ski trip is heavy-duty work. Just dressing the kids in their ski clothing is a giant ordeal. By the time I got them into their thermal socks, underwear, turtleneck sweaters, scarves, ski goggles, hats, and jackets, I was already close to exhaustion.

Heights are not my thing. The mere sight of a chair lift is enough to freak me out. I believe it's not natural for man to be suspended a hundred feet above an icy surface covered with boulders. I have serious doubts about trusting my life to some measly cable, which is the only thing separating me from certain death. Every year I watched in horror as my kids ascended a mountain the size of the Matterhorn, bonking each other on the head with their ski poles all the way up.

My kids weren't happy unless they're were hot-dogging all the way down a trail steeper than the monster roller coaster ride at Six Flags. I would stand there, holding my breath, as they flew down the hill at breakneck speed, jumping over moguls, snow flying all around them. And this was only after *one* lesson. Oy vey. And here I am, after three years of lessons, still at the bottom of the bunny slope, trying to figure out how to work the binders on my ski boots. I believe the expression that covers my behavior is *lame* or *lame-o*.

Rock Concerts

As early as eight and nine years old, kids are begging their parents to take them to these nighttime events. If you've never attended a rock concert, here's a word of caution. They are not one of your more wholesome activities for young kids. So you'll need to accompany them for at least the next decade. There is no other event that even comes close to what you'll experience at a rock concert. So, I only have two suggestions for you: earplugs and Advil.

Be prepared to see creatures that are straight from the bar scene of *Star Wars*. You'll see kids sporting spiky neon-colored hair, tattoos, and metal rings penetrating every conceivable inch of skin. These are kids whose only significant contribution to our society is in the field of body piercing. Before attending your first rock concert, here are some factoids to remember:

1. All rock bands have amps bigger than the World Trade Center capable of blowing out both your eustachian tubes before the end of the first riff.

2. Many kids attending these concerts are called "headbangers" because they keep the beat by

banging their heads against hard objects.[3] It does not take a rocket scientist to figure out that all headbangers are operating off their last two functioning brain cells.

3. The concert isn't considered a hit unless fifteen kids get crushed in the mosh pit.
4. The lead guitarist is in the habit of dropping acid and his pants throughout the entire concert.
5. The band members are so swamped by groupies, they have a roadie just to handle their condoms.

Expect to leave the concert with a paralyzing migraine. Your hair might even turn gray overnight. Other conditions like posttraumatic stress syndrome and shell shock can also occur. If your kids insist on mixing with deviants, you'd probably be safer taking them on a tour of the New York subways at two A.M.

Extreme Sporting Events

Your kids are probably into tennis, soccer, basketball, baseball, or football—or all of the above. Competitive sports are religion to all kids. And as their mom, you get the honor of schlepping them to all the practices besides their scheduled games. You'll spend most of your premenopausal years

---

3. The hardest being other kids' heads.

sitting on bleachers, watching your kids play in the most extreme weather conditions on earth. In the summer, there's the danger of dehydration and heat stroke. In the winter, hypothermia and frostbite. And that's just what *you're* in for—the kids will be fine.

But the real killer is the emotional wringer you're put through watching your kids play. Talk about nerves! Your stomach will be in knots all season. Every time your kid blows a play, you'll feel like blowing lunch. To help you get through this trauma, pack your sports bag with:

1. *Six-month supply of Tagamet*—It's either that or ulcerative colitis, take your pick.

2. *Ski mask*—You'll need a disguise after making a fool of yourself screaming obscenities at the coach.

3. *Portable I.V.*—When you become dehydrated after sitting on a sweltering baseball field for six straight hours, this is a quicker pick-me-up than Gatorade.

4. *Inflatable pillow*—To prevent calluses from forming on your buns after spending a season sitting on wooden bleachers.[4]

5. *Turkish towel*—To sop up the gallons of tears you'll shed after every heartbreaking loss.

---

4. Tweezers aren't a bad idea, either.

Disneyland

Every parent knows he'll have to make this pilgrimage at least once a year. Disneyland is touted as "the most fun place on earth." But a more accurate statement would be "the most expensive place on earth." So make several trips to the ATM before you go. For openers, the admission is a staggering ninety-five dollars per inch of kid. Then you have to stand for hours in incredibly long lines, constructed like rat mazes. A rule of thumb: For every three hours you stand in line, you'll get three seconds of ride.

Every supergerm and virus known to man is being carried by some dufus in line. In my opinion, you should get fully immunized before you step one foot into the place. You'll be forced to stand next to people who act like they're suffering from mad cow disease. They also look like they need to be put to sleep. They're hacking, wheezing, and spitting up all kinds of stuff. And none of them uses a handkerchief either.[5] It's no surprise that Michael Jackson wears a surgical mask while stalking at the park.

Everything about this place gives you a headache. From the nauseating rides that scramble your inner ear to the thirty-dollar Goofy and Mickey T-shirts your kids continually nag

---

5. They're wearing them as bandannas.

you to buy. By the end of the day, you've got legal grounds for euthanasia.

Top Ten Most Common Sights at Disneyland

1. Tank tops and tattoos
2. Wedgies[6]
3. Totally trashed restrooms
4. Vending machines dispensing antibiotics
5. Parents gulping down Xanax
6. People using barf bags
7. Churros taller than Mary Lou Retton
8. Dogs and kids wearing muzzles
9. Ritalin kiosks
10. Achy-breaky hairdos

6. Not the shoes, either.

Mom's Ten Commandments:

Holy House Arrest!

Okay, everybody still living at home—front and center! Pay
attention. I am about to save your life. Because if you don't do
what I tell you, your mom is going to kill you. I am listing all
the stuff that you do that drives your moms nuts! And don't
try to sneak out before reading it thoroughly. You think you
can get off that easy? You guys don't live on an island where
there are no rules. Remember, even Rudy and Gretchen got
booted off their island in the end. So don't push your luck.

Here are the rules. They're also going to be strictly
enforced. Any infraction of them could get you twenty-five to
life. So shape up and quit your crying, or I'll really give you
something to cry about!

Boy, did that feel good. My kids are all grown up now, so I haven't been able to yell at them like that for a real long time.[1] Now, I am sure that none of you would ever think of breaking any of the original Ten Commandments. If you do, you know you will have to answer to a higher authority—like Charlton Heston, who will come down from the Hollywood Hills and take you out with his biblical AK-47.

It's time to get out your highlighter and be prepared for a quiz on Mom's Ten Commandments. And don't question us why you have to obey them. The answer is always the same: *Because we said so.*

Mom's Ten Commandments

1. *Close the door—don't slam it!*—Why? Because when a kid slams the door, it sends shock waves down our spines of an intensity not felt since Hiroshima. Remember: All moms' nerves are strung tighter than Itzhak Perlman's violin. So that unexpected slamming noise really makes us go ballistic.

   It also scares the crap out of the dog—literally. It is the number one[2] cause of every one of his white-carpet accidents. Then we are forced to

---

1. Two weeks.
2. Pun intended.

spend the entire afternoon on our hands and knees with a toothbrush, a bottle of stain remover, and a really bad attitude.

2. *The refrigerator is not to be used as a locker.*—So we are asking you to please take all of your personal effects out of there, including the:

   • six tubes of L'Oréal Lip Pulp
   • film for your photography club
   • angora sweaters
   • dissected animals from your biology class
   • lunch bag you forgot back in 1997 and is now covered with mutated mold
   • corsage from last year's prom

   You ask why do you need to remove these things? Because we are left with no room to store incidentals, like, oh, let's say—food.

3. *Do not put Coca-Cola cans in the freezer to "quick chill" them.*—We mothers know from years of experience that, without a doubt, you will forget that you put them in there. And fifteen minutes after you leave the house, the cans will freeze and explode, spewing thirty-six ounces of sticky, gelid Coke all over the frozen foods, the wire shelves, and the inside of the door. F.Y.I—it takes approximately six and a half months to get this frozen slush out of every crevice it's seeped into.

We also don't want to sustain a severe case of frostbite while we're in the freezer trying to clean your mess up, thank you. We already get that every winter when your dad tries to save money by turning down the thermostat.

4. *Your friends must come to the front door to pick you up.*— They are not allowed to sit in the driveway, honking their horns. Why? Because we know for a certainty that you are still in the shower, haven't picked out the clothes you are going to wear, and will make at least thirty-three phone calls before you're ready to go. This means that your friends will be out there for approximately thirty-six hours before they even see your sorry face.

    Also, don't forget that you have several neighbors who are avid duck hunters—regular card-carrying members of the NRA who carry a picture of Charlton Heston in their wallets. So don't be surprised when they fire a couple of rounds on your honking friends to try and thin out the flock.

5. *You will not leave the house looking like that!*—This is your cue to say, "Like what? I'm dressed okay." Really? We don't think so. You guys had better change those rap pants that are huge enough to conceal Iraq's entire arsenal of weapons. And you, girl. You won't be able to conceal anything

with what little you've got on. We mean it, literally, when we say "get dressed." Put some clothes on. You are not going anywhere looking like Lil' Kim in a thong and matching pastie. You're going to school, not the MTV Awards.

6. *Hang up your clothes!*—Remember those things called hangers? And no—they're not where you park a plane. The hangers in your closet are to hang your clothes on! *Du-uu-uh.* You kids live under the misguided impression that your bedroom floor is to be used in place of your closet and dresser drawers. So this is our rule: If you don't pick that pile of clothes up off the floor so we can get a vacuum in there, we're going to use it as a Flo-Bee to cut your hair.

   Also, if you expect us to make your beds every day, we have to find them first. Going into your room is like entering *The Twilight Zone.*[3] The bed has disappeared into some third dimension and killer bacteria lurk everywhere in the piles of filthy clothes.

7. *Don't tell us not to touch your stuff.*—Kids constantly complain that when we clean their rooms, we rearrange their stuff and they can't find anything

---

3. Rod Serling declined this episode.

anymore. Get serious. Like, is there some demented "system" you have perfected where the papers strewn all over the floor, the clothes under the bed, the books under the bedspread, and the six gazillion CDs randomly thrown around the room are in "order"?

Well, let me give you a news flash. The Navy couldn't find a nuclear sub in your room without the help of sophisticated radar and infrared imaging equipment. Even then, it could take years.

8. *You are forbidden to date any alleged life form who shows up:*
   - with spiky hair dyed to match his neon bike shorts
   - wearing a Megadeth T-shirt, picturing the band eating live rodents
   - wearing gobs of eye shadow, mascara, and lipstick[4]
   - with more studs embedded on his tongue than on his leather jacket
   - announcing he is there to pick up his "booty call"

9. *Don't crank up the volume on your CD players and radios.*—We have all suffered enough hearing loss

---

4. That goes for guys, too.

already. For God's sake, as it is, we have to scream at each other to be heard. How much more eardrum damage must we sustain? Will the next step be "signing"?

Also, quit serenading the neighbors from your car radio at two A.M. to the melodic strains of Eminem, Puff Daddy, and Snoop Doggy Dog. Remember, disturbing the peace is punishable by a jail sentence. One day, you may end up sharing a cell with all these guys. And make no mistake: No matter when you go, they'll be there.

10. *Respect your curfew.*—If you're lying awake nights trying to think of clever schemes to fool us, don't even bother. We're quite aware of any tricks you might employ to try and sneak in past your curfew hour. There isn't anything you can come up with that we haven't already tried ourselves. Among them are:

- slipping the dog some Sominex[5] so he won't bark when you come in at two A.M.
- sleeping over at friends' home whose parents both work the night shift
- crawling in your bedroom window at six A.M., then coming to breakfast like you just got up and dressed

---

5. Or your dad and me, either.

- creating some minor diversion to take the attention off you when you come in at three A.M.—like calling in a bomb scare

Okay, you can be excused now. I think we understand each other. And you should know that if you break any of these commandments, your punishment will be fair—like burning in the fires of hell for eternity. Have a nice day.

Teenage Tactics Quiz

1. Show your kids that you trust them. Never go through their personal effects, sniffing around for drugs. A better method is to:
   a. talk candidly with your kids about them
   b. have them sign a nonuse drug contract
   c. educate them through antidrug videos
   d. let a police dog do it

2. For their ultimate well-being, shield them for as long as possible from:
   a. your marital spats
   b. foul language
   c. any act of violence
   d. any episode of *Sex and the City*

3. In order to prevent a senseless death by violence, your kid should never:
    a. be allowed to own a gun
    b. be allowed to join a gang
    c. be allowed to drive through bad neighborhoods
    d. let you catch him having sex

4. Most fatal teenage accidents occur:
    a. while driving drunk
    b. when jaywalking
    c. when speeding
    d. in mosh pits

5. A teenage boy's first sexual experience usually happens:
    a. on prom night
    b. when he's been drinking
    c. when he's fifteen
    d. when he's on-line

6. The one thing in a teenager's room that is never opened is:
    a. a dictionary
    b. a math book
    c. his set of encyclopedias
    d. his dirty clothes hamper

7. For his prom, it's customary for the boy to rent which of the following?
   a. his tuxedo
   b. his dress shoes
   c. the limo
   d. the hotel room

8. Nowadays, kids don't dislike or fear their teachers like they used to. Instead, they:
   a. identify with their goals
   b. use many as role models
   c. treat them with great respect
   d. date them

The answer to all questions is *d* as in *don't do it*.
7–8 right: You did good.
4–6 right: Slap on the hand.
0–3 right: Doomed as doomed can be.

CHAPTER
12

Addicted Moms:

Women Behaving Badly

Everybody has their day in court. Moms are put on trial the day their kids wake up to the fact that their friends are all having a lot more fun doing things that you won't allow them to do. When they finally come to this realization, be prepared to hear them complain on a daily basis: "You never let me do anything. I never have any fun. My life sucks."

Oh, yeah? Believe me, it works both ways. Nowadays, in our politically correct society, moms also have to give up a lot of the things they enjoy, just because of the kids. Well, sort of . . . like smoking, for one. Lots of women really try like crazy to give it up, but it's just not that easy. So they become "sneak smokers" to hide it from their kids. The coverups, the plots, the red herrings—it's more work than trying to hide an affair.[1]

Political correctness can be such a bummer. When I was raising my kids twenty years ago, everybody and his brother smoked. Nobody made such a big deal over it like they do today. These days, it's practically against the law to smoke in public. If you light up anywhere, you're arrested, cuffed, and dragged away in front of your horrified children. Then, you've got to attend some kind of rehab program for six months. Give me a break. Back in the '70s, smoking was not only legal, it was compulsory.

But nowadays, the antismoking crusaders have made the whole country more paranoid than Keith Richards at a law enforcement rally. They have waged a vitriolic campaign, making "our children" the victims.

Their witch hunt has targeted Joe Camel as the devil incarnate who will lead our children astray. As a result, he has been banned from magazine ads and billboards all over the country. Poor Joe. If I were him, I'd run like hell back to the desert. This group won't rest until he's publicly neutered.

It's this kind of climate that has forced moms to become closet smokers. Literally. When girlfriends visit for a cup of coffee, they hide from the kids by gathering in the bathroom to sneak their ciggies. They stay in there for hours, alternately

---

1. Just ask any White House intern.

gabbing and blowing all that smoke out of one tiny window. It's a miracle one of the neighbors doesn't see it and call the fire department.

Every few minutes one of the moms emerges to make sure the kids are still playing nicely and nobody has killed anybody. After they're finished, they conveniently flush all the butts down the toilet. The neat part is that the kids are clueless about what their moms are doing in there. They all grow up thinking that it's normal for women to go to the bathroom in groups.

And please don't lecture us! We're subjected to enough of them as it is, from the peanut gallery:

Emotional: Your kid throws himself at your feet, sobbing and screaming, "Mommy's gonna die—Mommy's gonna die!"

Moral: Your ten-year-old gets on his soapbox and delivers a fire and brimstone sermon about the evils of smoking: "It not only damages your heart and circulatory system, but increases your incidences of lung cancer . . . three hundred thousand deaths are caused annually by blah, blah, blah."

Legal: Your children retain a lawyer and sue you for the damages incurred by your secondhand smoke.

All I know is one thing. Between the kids and the reformed smokers with their holier-than-thou attitude, smokers are less welcome than O.J. anywhere they go. Even the Hare Krishnas have more rights at the airports.

If an adult lights up in someone's home, they'd better count on the fact that they are going to have to tolerate somebody's two-year-old screaming: *"No—no! Smoking bad for you!"* Excuse me, I don't think so. The smoke may be obnoxious, but so is the kid's behavior. And anyway, who is he to talk? He needs to spend the afternoon in an enclosed room, inhaling the fumes from his own diaper pail.

In the process of trying to hide their bad habits, moms have come up with some pretty ingenious places to hide their ciggies:

1. in the freezer
2. inside their bra cups[2]
3. in their Tampax boxes
4. taped to the underside of the sink

Okay, let's talk about the real health risks. The biggest risk is developing bronchitis. But it's not from the cigarettes. It's from having to go outdoors to sneak a puff or two in nothing but a thin cotton house robe. You stand there, often in thity-two-degree weather, shivering like a chihuahua. To hell with the mailmen. Smokers have to brave the rain, sleet, and snow for their cause and don't get to shoot anybody, either. The truth is that moms who smoke run a greater risk of dying from exposure than any lung disease.

Smoking moms have learned to fabricate more coverups than the Clinton administration. They are constantly interrogated by their kids, who have olfactory lobes as keen as bloodhounds: "Mom, is that *smoke* I smell, smoke on your clothes?" So

2. B cups only hold half a pack.

we live with a bottle of Binaca and spritz gallons of perfume on ourselves. We use car deodorizers and fabric fresheners, fumigating every inch of space we inhabit. Forget the fact that our husbands, kids, and dogs spend every evening tooting out toxic gas from their Del Taco burritos. This is acceptable. But a little cigarette smoke and they're, like, so offended.

It's always the same story. Just when you think you have perfected all your subterfuges, one of your kids walks into the room unexpectedly and catches you in the act of enjoying your Virginia Slim. Bam. You're so busted! So he yells, "Mom —what are you *doing?* You're gonna be in *big trouble* when Dad comes home!" Talk about your words coming back to haunt you. And there's not much you can do in your own defense, either. You just have to sit there, looking guiltier than one of the bozos on *Judge Judy.*

Another potentially addictive situation is the "girls' night out." It starts innocently enough when you decide to celebrate one of your girlfriends' birthdays. It's about the only opportunity a mom gets to ditch the kids for a few hours and kick up her heels a little. And what better way to "celebrate" that special occasion than in a drunken stupor with your friends? Your only downfall is that if you've got a lot of girl-friends, you'll end up "celebrating" twice a week.[3]

---

3. At Betty Ford, eventually.

The evenings start out with giggly, girly-gossip over a nice dinner and a few glasses of wine. But after the fourth glass of Pinot Grigio, you've all passed the point of no return. You have just entered the Maudlin Zone. This is when gals get all weepy and slobber on and on about how much they love each other and each other's kids. After the third round of samboucas and espresso, you're at the "If I were to get a terminal disease, I'd want you girls to take care of my kids" thing. Oh, man. Watch out for this stage. It's sloppier than baby drool and accompanied by more blubber than a Sumo wrestler.

Another occasion that can get a gal into big trouble is a Saturday afternoon baby shower. It begins demurely enough, with finger sandwiches and a glass of champagne. However, by the time the mom-to-be gets through opening her huge pile of baby gifts, you're sipping your fifth glass. As you crawl home at two P.M. doing 15 mph, you're wondering how you are going to get through the door without running into your kids. So you tippy-toe past the family room, where they're watching TV, hoping to make it upstairs before they see you. But no such luck. This is when your daughter sees you and gives you plenty of that junior-high attitude. You can't put anything over on her—she's sharp as a tack.

"Geez, Mom. You're a mess! You'd better get upstairs in bed before Daddy sees you."

That's your cue to try as hard as you can to speak without slurring and walk without tripping. But no can do. At this point, you're weaving more than a Fruit of the Loom factory.

Somehow you make it up the stairs to your bathroom and splash cold water on your face. Then you open the window for some fresh air to clear your head. Now you figure as long as the window is open, you might as well have just one ciggie to calm your nerves. But just this one time, because you promised yourself you're quitting tomorrow—after your girls' night out, of course.

Is there a problem with that? What's the big deal? We girls just want to have fun!

Rate Your Addiction Quiz

True or False

1. You have been known to start kitchen fires in order to camouflage your cigarette smoke.

2. Your husband enrolls you in behavior modification classes along with the family shih tzu.

3. The girlfriends and you don't mind taking an outdoor table at your favorite restaurant in the middle of a tornado watch so you can smoke.

4. Growing up, alcoholism was considered a career goal in your family.

5. You're only flying to Korea these days, because it's the one airline left that still allows their passengers to smoke.

6. In order to avoid looking like a serious drinker, you always order a drink with an umbrella in it.

7. Since you have rationed yourself to five cigarettes a day, you have taken up smoking those 120s that are so long they need a splint to support them.

8. Besides celebrating birthdays, weddings, babies, and anniversaries, your girls'-night-out group is now adding ovulation to the list.

9. For your birthday, the family has chipped in for a gift certificate to Betty Ford.

10. You figured out a way to cut your smoking down to only one pack per year. From now on, you're only going to smoke after sex.

Score 1 addiction point for every *T* answer.

0–4: Mary Poppins knockoff.

5–7: Betty Ford candidate.

8–10: Hard time with Robert Downey.

CHAPTER

13

Dating Moms:

Who's Your Daddy?

Fact: More than 50 percent of the marriages in this country end up in divorce. That's a pretty grim stat, isn't it? Every year, millions of marriages hit those rough seas and end up sinking to the bottom of the ocean. Luckily all the divorce lawyers are already down there with the rest of the bottom feeders, so you can get immediate assistance. Either by choice or because we're given no choice, our lives as wives and mothers can change in an instant.

One day you're Donna Reed, dressed in your frilly apron and pearl choker, baking cookies in the kitchen. The next thing you know, you're parading your spandex-clad butt around a singles bar. You'll be showing more curves than life is throwing you.

Be prepared for the consequences of your actions! Your kids are going to go into a tailspin. They'll be more out of control than Robert Downey on parole. Why? First of all, they'll be absolutely horrified at their "new" mom and her new, swinging lifestyle.

What's more, they're going to go nuts every time they hear the word *baby-sitter*. When a woman is dating a different guy every night, it's a given that the baby-sitter is going to be the ersatz mom for quite a while. Maybe you'd better just hand your kids an autographed eight-by-ten glossy to remember you by. Between the string of baby-sitters and new men you're bringing home, the kids are going to feel like their house is filled with more aliens than Tattouweim.

Most divorced women are totally terrified at the prospect of having to go through the dating thing again. It's like taking two giant steps backward. Trust me. I had to do it—and it was torture. Also, divorce favors no particular age. Single moms are always on the lookout for potential stepdad candidates. Many women in their twenties on up suddenly find themselves at the Saturday night Parents Without Partners dances desperately seeking a man of marriageable material. The problem is, the ones they come across are all cut from the same cloth—cheesecloth. When any one of these "eligible men" asks you to dance, you'll discover the only thing he's interested in doing is the horizontal polka.

• • •

So where else can a divorced woman go to find single guys hanging out? Ugh, don't ask. Her dismal choices are:

1. *The 'Net*—Who wants to spend their weekends in those dismal chat rooms with a gazillion losers who all log on under the name "Studmuffin"? Chances are that most of them aren't even single. Chances are even better that most of them aren't even guys.

2. *Getting fixed up*—You swore off blind dates years ago when your mother fixed you up with a washing-machine repairman that she tried to pass off as a "mechanical engineer."

3. *The grocery store*—Chances are that any guy who spends all his free time hanging around the produce counter squeezing melons is a registered sex offender.

So what happens is most women take their chances looking for love in one of those dreaded singles bars. The female primal urge to be partnered up for life is a strong one, so she goes on the prowl in this habitat with worse dating material than the NFL. Divorced women are forever trying to fill up an emotional hole bigger than the one in the ozone layer. But their choices are very limited. They can either tough it out at one of those horrible meat markets or get butchered in the supermarket.

A word of advice before entering the place—lower your expectations. The singles bar scene is going to be just like the one from *Star Wars*. You're going to meet more bad characters than Jar Jar Binks. Let me go out on a limb here. The kinds of guys who hang out in singles bars aren't any prizes.[1] Some women test the waters by going to less threatening places like the karaoke bars. Personally, I think these places are a really bad idea because they combine two evils: people who shouldn't drink with people who shouldn't sing.

When you first walk into a singles bar, don't be alarmed when a flash of light temporarily blinds you. It's only the reflection from hundreds of gold chains on the aging men hanging out at the bar. Get ready for a bunch of middle-aged guys who have thinning hair on their heads but sport clumps of it hanging from their chests and ears.[2] Gross out. It helps to think of all those receding hairlines as the site of future hair plugs.

Also, check out those huge metal belt buckles they wear with their low-slung jeans. That's an accident waiting to happen. Don't ever ask them to bend over and pick up your purse. One false move and they could easily castrate themselves. On second thought—aw, go ahead!

When you finally bring one of these critters home to meet the kids, you're not going to get off without hearing at least one scarcastic remark like: "Hey, Mom. Where did you dig up the Elvis impersonator?"

The name game is a deciding factor for getting a date in a singles bar. Besides the fact that there are more Tonys in singles

---

1. Except booby.
2. You may have to use sign language to communicate.

bars than in southern Italy, they all want to date girls with names of lamps, like Tiffany. Also, most of these men are really emotionally battered head cases. These guys are carrying more baggage than United Airlines. Plus, they're not only going through divorces but midlife crises, too.

You can spot them right away because they're the ones with the bonded teeth who date stewardesses. These men are still reeling emotionally, physically, and financially from getting brutalized in the divorce courts. Remember, the Latin root of the word *divorce* means "ripping a man's genitals out through his wallet." You're dealing with a segment of the population who share the common belief that all women are greedy, evil bitches.[3]

Don't kid yourselves. Most of these men are just out to get you in the sack with no emotional commitment. At this point, sex is all it's about for them. The qualifications for a good bed partner don't include knowing the difference between right and wrong—just between right and left.

They also prefer a girl half their age or less and would actually prefer her to be a virgin. They claim the reason is that they don't want the responsibility of the kids that come with the package. But that's a lot of bull. The real reason they all want virgins is that they can't stand criticism. So that leaves all the divorced women out in the cold. The last time

---

3. And those are their good points.

most of us were virgins, the Louisiana Purchase was still in escrow.

If you do suffer a temporary psychotic episode and happen to end up with one of these cradle robbers, don't let him within a mile of your teenage daughter. He might just try to make a pass for her. And the one man you don't need in your life is Woody Allen. So the big question women need to ask themselves before considering any serious relationship will be: Is this the man I want my children to spend their weekends with?

It's beyond depressing. The single mom is going to feel that a good man is harder to locate than Dennis Rodman after his wedding. You'll get to the point where just the mere thought of having to go through that dog-and-pony show at the bar scene every night will be a major turn-off. All those boring conversations, the sexual games—the whole thing is exhausting. It would be a lot easier to stand in the parking lot and hand out your résumé.

Competing with all the younger gals out there is a real challenge. Before I got divorced, I used to wear clothing that was so baggy you could hide a major appliance in there. But I quickly learned I'd have to trade in my sweats for rib-crunching bustiers and clingy spandex dresses. When you arrive at this fashion destination, be prepared for a strong reaction from your kids—like throwing a sheet over you when you're out in public with them. Also be prepared for some more of their "cute" remarks like: "Mom, you sure look like a doll tonight—Dominatrix Barbie."

And while we're on the subject of Barbie, every fifty-year-old menopausal divorcée knows that the eligible guys her age all want to date a Barbie doll—even if she is Wild Mood Swing Barbie.

You also have to play the game and not come across as too intelligent. They're looking for a woman whose biggest literary accomplishment is getting through the Sears catalog. Basically, the divorced men who hang out at singles bars only have two qualifications for dating a woman: thin with big boobs. The only thing lower than their IQs is their standards.

Ten Useful Guy Factoids

1. You might as well date a guy much younger than yourself. It takes them forever to grow up anyway.
2. Most guys are like place mats. They only show up when food is on the table.
3. The relationship is definitely over when you begin correcting each other's grammar during sex.
4. If some guy criticizes you by saying that you don't show enough interest in his family, date his brother.
5. If you're waiting for him to pop the Big Question— don't get too excited. The only question he's going to pop is—shouldn't you be seeing other people?

6. A guy is basically as faithful as his options.

7. A ménage à trois is a man's way of saying, "You complete me."

8. Most men you meet at karaoke bars have the personality of ZIP codes in Kansas.

9. Basically, the only difference between a husband and a boyfriend is forty-five minutes.

10. A rich man is not necessarily smarter than a poor man. A good example of that is Donald Trump. The only things denser than his eyebrows are his dates.

CHAPTER
14

"Empty Nest Syndrome" Moms:

For the Birds

They say that one of the first signs of mental illness is dressing up your pets. Guilty as charged. But it's not because I'm nuts—at least I don't think so. This wacko practice started after both of my kids left home for college. It's not schizophrenia. It's called the empty nest syndrome. And, believe me, it's true. After my boys flew the coop for college, my nest was emptier than a politician's promises.

After acting as chief cook, bottle washer, and Machiavellian drill sergeant for twenty years, I thought it would be wonderful to get some solitude. But I got more than I bargained for—

my house went from Grand Central Station to the last stop at Clarkesville.

The first month was the worst. I became restless, pacing from room to room, at a loss for what to do with myself. I was irritable all the time and too old to blame it on PMS. I'd turn on the TV and one of those Kodak "Times of Your Life" commercials would be showing some happy family gathered around the fireplace, while schmaltzy music swelled in the background. Then I'd lose it—cry like a baby.[1]

I knew I'd have to find some sort of emotional replacement for my absentee kids. So I turned my sights toward my flea-bitten dog, Flatulous Rex, whom I had ignored for years. He stayed outdoors in his little doghouse, living a kind of hippie existence for the past six years. You can imagine his confusion when all of a sudden, I brought him into the house, bathed him, and started calling him my baby. What's worse, I took to dressing him in little sweaters with matching bonnets and paraded him around the neighborhood.

Naturally, the dog totally freaked. He just couldn't handle it and suffered a massive identity crisis. He refused to eat any kind of dog food and began throwing temper tantrums. I had to put him into doggie therapy, but he's doing much better now. I think he's actually beginning to enjoy our little talks we have in the afternoons when I give him his bottle. I

---

1. The acting was that bad.

know he certainly enjoys being pushed in the stroller, that's for sure.

For the first few months after the boys left home, I hated to go into their rooms. When I did, I'd get all misted up at the sight of those empty rooms with made-up beds and clean floors. I missed the old rooms that looked like war-torn areas of Bosnia. I even missed the rap music blaring from boom-boxes the size of Cleveland. Everything was so pristine and quiet. It creeped me out. But what was even creepier was my behavior. I began talking to the pictures of my kids like it was really them. I could have been Bruce Willis in *The Sixth Sense.*[2]

There's nothing more dangerous than a woman with a lot of time on her hands. You can get into a lot of trouble, trust me. You get into the daily habit of doing lunch with the girls and then gossiping over the bridge table until 6 P.M. You end up playing cards seven days a week, pigging out on avocado dip and Cheetos. Pretty soon, your butt becomes so wide they could show *How the West Was Won* on it. Plus, you develop a mouth nastier than Morton Downey Jr's. It got so bad, I couldn't even stand being in a room with myself anymore.

I decided it was high time to do a complete overhaul of my life and fill it with productive activities. When the kids were home, my life revolved around making school lunches, carpooling, PTA meetings, and staying awake half the night

---

2. However, I would have preferred being Demi in *Striptease.*

on weekends worrying until the boys got home. With all of this gone, I realized I'd have to make more adjustments than a chiropractor. But I was ready and willing.

Here are some of the changes I made in my life:

My Car

When I was lugging a bunch of boys around, my car was always loaded up with soccer gear, tennis racquets, and cases of Dr Pepper. I didn't need a car, I needed an army vehicle. So I drove this huge, suburban Humvee assault vehicle that was as wide as my parents' motor home in Florida. This vehicle could have been used for reconnaissance missions in war-torn third world countries, but it worked great for me. My Humvee was ten feet wide and could take out three garage doors in a matter of seconds.

Hauling kids around, you need something that can withstand the constant assault of hockey sticks, Super-soakers, and hundreds of elbow jabs. Mothers spend the greater part of their lives in their cars, chauffeuring their kids to and from all kinds of activities. We need something we can practically live in because we're on the road more than Willie Nelson.

So I traded Big Bertha in for a dainty, new Honda Civic. But it took some getting used to. I had to change my whole perspective. It was the first time in a decade I actually drove a car where I wasn't sitting eighteen feet above the highway.

It was also really weird backing up without hearing that beeping noise all the time. But the best part was that this car didn't constantly reek of gamy gym socks.

Cooking

For years I felt like Hop Sing on the Ponderosa. Cooking for three men doesn't exactly require a degree from the Cordon Bleu. We're talking about guys here. They consider a gourmet restaurant any place with a drive-up window. They actually prefer their burgers with the grill marks painted on them. Quality never mattered—only quantity.

After the boys left, I got to replace the pizza, tacos, and corn dogs with foodstuffs that actually had some nutritional value. I spread my culinary wings and experimented with a whole variety of new dishes. They were met with rave reviews by my husband and Flatulous Rex. It was really nice to get some accolades in the kitchen after such a long time. The one time I tried cooking a fancy dish for the boys, all I heard was, "Ugh! What *is* this junk? Do we have to eat it? It tastes like barf!" Gee, thanks, guys. *Bon appétit* to you, too.

Hobbies

It was definitely time to develop some type of fulfilling hobby for myself. But what should it be? I decided to try flea marketing on weekends in search of collectibles. I figured this was a great ongoing project to keep my mind occupied. But my mind didn't need occupation, it needed rehabilitation, as evidenced by the high-priced junk I brought home:

1. Legends of NASCAR commemorative plates
2. assortment of pink Depression glass dishes[3]
3. souvenir teaspoons from every theme park in America
4. complete collection of '50s Frankie Yankovic polka albums
5. one-of-a-kind Barbie dolls[4]
6. reproductions of all the art in Graceland
7. multiple sets of tarnished fish knives
8. assorted hotel napkins bearing logos and multiple coffee stains
9. six boxes of moldy, water-damaged *Spider Man* comic books
10. four dozen unmatched, chipped demitasse cups and saucers

---

3. Diagnosed as clinically depressed.
4. Dominatrix Barbie and PMS Barbie.

Computer

My next project was to become totally computer savvy and join ranks with millions of other cybergeeks. My goal was to go on-line and learn as much as possible about ancient Rome. But a funny thing happened on the way to the Colosseum. I got waylaid in the chat rooms.

Although they claim to be harmless, I found out that they're more addictive than beer and Beanie Babies. In fact, they should have AA meetings for them. I would sit down at the computer at eight A.M. in my housecoat with a cup of coffee, and the next thing I knew it was eight P.M. I hadn't even gotten up to go to the bathroom, get dressed, or comb my hair. I looked like a homeless woman. What's worse, my husband was so unhappy with me, I was about to become one.

My husband finally issued an ultimatum: The computer or the curb. I think that secretly he was afraid I was spending time in those sex chat rooms. Why would I want to do this? I never even mastered the art of regular sex all that well. Even if I wanted to have cybersex, I'd probably type too quickly.

Golf

This seemed to be the answer to my prayers. First of all, it filled up my time. It takes roughly three months to play a round of golf. Second, my husband and I could play together or with other couples. This made him happy and it gave us a nice social life, too. Now, I wouldn't say I exactly took to it like a duck to water. At first, I put more balls in the water than the men's Olympic swimming team. But I knew I was going to make it the day they let me remove the handicap sticker from my golf cart.

Empty Nest Quiz

1. Your kids will consider your weekly visits to see them on campus as:
   a. good parenting
   b. normal curiosity
   c. supportive
   d. stalking

2. When your kids send home their dirty laundry from college, the first thing you should do is:
   a. send it to the dry cleaners
   b. wash it in hot water with bleach
   c. wash it in the heavy-duty cycle
   d. nuke it

3. The best remedy for getting rid of those empty nest blues is:

   a. volunteer work

   b. physical exercise

   c. a sugar-free diet

   d. Zoloft

4. Which hobby best remedies the empty nest syndrome?

   a. reading

   b. gardening

   c. painting

   d. kidnapping

5. When your kids run out of clean clothes at college, how will they get their dirty laundry home to you?

   a. by FedEx

   b. by UPS

   c. via U.S. Postal Service

   d. The clothes will get up and walk home by themselves.

6. With a minimum of work, you can turn your kid's old room into a:
   a. sewing room
   b. exercise room
   c. library
   d. shrine

7. When your husband requests breakfast in bed after the kids go away to college, tell him to:
   a. let you know the night before
   b. send you flowers
   c. reciprocate the next week
   d. sleep in the kitchen

8. When your son leaves for college, what is the first thing you will throw away?
   a. his old clothes
   b. his high school books
   c. his worn-out sneakers
   d. your alarm clock

9. What crime will a grown son never forgive his mother for?

   a. not paying for grad school

   b. not accepting his fiancée

   c. not allowing him to play football in high school

   d. throwing away his collection of comic books

10. The day the last kid leaves for college, what will your husband go out and buy for the two of you?

    a. a sports car

    b. an expensive dinner

    c. a vacation home

    d. love toys

Results of your ENQ (Empty Nest Quiz):

   Score 1 point for every correct *d* answer.

   8–10 right: The nest is half full.

   4–7 right: The nest is half empty.

   0–3 right: The nest is history.

Change of Life Moms:

Inconceivable

Women are having babies much later in life than a few decades ago. There are a lot of practical reasons behind this trend, too. Nowadays, couples need two salaries to keep up with the astronomical cost of buying homes, cars, and a Starbucks nonfat mocha latte. Most women find they just can't afford to give up that extra income, so it's becoming commonplace to delay pregnancy until their late thirties or forties.

But eventually, there comes the time when you've got to get off the proverbial pot and get a move on. We gals aren't in the egg business indefinitely. Our biological clocks are ticking along, as evidenced by the expiration date stamped above each ovary. Also, if you wait much beyond forty, you'll need an ob/mag[1] instead of an ob/gyn. When you've reached the time of life where your periods are more irregular than the clothes at Kmart, it's nature's way of telling you that time is running out.

However, one reason women are able to put off childbearing is that now we have other means available to us. New advances in medicine have given us many exciting new options in the field of child conception. There are new technologies that make it possible for single women, women with infertile partners, and even postmenopausal women to bear children. Nowadays, nothing is impossible. There are sixty-year-old women out there having babies. And no matter how hopeless your situation may seem, you can always log on to www.no chance in hell.com to find your miracle. Not to mention the weekly auctions for eggs and sperm on eBay. Plus, if you're over sixty, you've got the added bonus of Medicare paying for it. And even if they don't, you can always count on the *National Enquirer*.

If a woman is incapable of a normal conception, she still has these options:

1. being artificially inseminated with her husband's sperm
2. insemination from an anonymous donor[2]

---

1. Obstetrician/magician.
2. Later revealed to be David Crosby.

3. insemination via turkey baster
4. implantation with her own eggs, which were previously frozen
5. waging a court battle where Judge Judy awards custody of someone else's eggs

Often, the baby can be delivered naturally with only an epidural anesthetic. Many older women have kept themselves in such good physical shape that a natural delivery isn't that risky.[3] However, if the doctor foresees any problems, a cesarean section is always a safe alternative.

Older women also have the choice of delivering in a birthing chair, by Lamaze, or even by the LeBoyer method, where the baby is born in a tub of warm water. My personal opinion? All this high-tech stuff is making the whole process just a little too weird. I know we are in the twilight years, but this is more like *The Twilight Zone*. Remember, it's not nice to fool Mother Nature. Are we really up to this? Call me old-fashioned, but I think that a woman should have a baby the way God intended—strapped on a table, numb from the waist down.

So where do you go shopping for eggs when you're fresh out, yourself? The Internet, where else? You can find all kinds of eggs for sale on the 'Net, with good credentials from the donors. One recent Web site (www.eggsRus.com) boasts that

---

3. Or even an unnatural one.

it has eggs harvested from the ovaries of young supermodels. Is this a good idea? Have we become so superficial that we would go to such lengths to produce only children who are as beautiful as supermodels? That's scary. What's even scarier is if the baby grows up to have the *brains* of a supermodel.

Today, doctors say that a woman in basically good health is a good candidate to have a baby well into her fifties and sixties. Oh, sure. They also tell you that everything is in your head, too. The real problem is where the heck are you going to get enough energy to function as a new mom at that age? How will you ever manage to run after a toddler all day long? And what about ten years from now? Will you be able to play sports like baseball and tennis with your kid? I've got one word for you—*osteoporosis*. At your age, anywhere you get hit you break your hip.

But can you imagine the torture of going through the change of life with all the PMS involved *and* being pregnant, too? Two words—*Apocalypse Now*. Between the mood swings, morning sickness, and water retention, even Gandhi would be unable to live with you. It's a foregone conclusion that you're going to become a terrorist who holds everyone in your family hostage for nine months. As a matter of fact, your family would have better luck negotiating with the real thing.

What about the consequences of the sixty-year age difference? While your kid is watching *Barney* videos, you'll be watching stuff like *Rocky VII: Fighting Incontinence.* Also what kind of life is it, always being the oldest mom at all the school functions? Who likes having to sit there in orthopedic hose and rubber underpants, while all the other mothers are wearing Lycra bodysuits?

I still haven't made up my mind about all the medical advances available to women. On one hand, it is a blessing to many women past forty who really want to have kids. On the other, I still have more reservations than the Red Lobster on Saturday night. I wouldn't want to hang out with a bunch of elderly moms and be constantly gawked at. I can just hear the catty remarks from the younger women. Among other things, you know they're saying your group looks like the road company from *Cocoon.*

Besides the problem of being physically able to keep up, what about mentally? You know what those "senior moments" are like. What if you are getting ready to go to the supermarket and leave the baby in his car seat on the roof of your car? Believe me, you don't want to keep screwing up with stunts like that and have your kid spend all his formative years being mad at you. Remember, he's the one who will be choosing your rest home in the near future.

What about twenty years down the road, when it's time for your kid to get married? You'll be well into your seventies. Just think about a wedding with all your seventy-year-old pals in attendance. Your kids will look at the group and tell you they've seen younger faces on money. It sure seems like there are a lot more negatives than positives when considering this late-in-life pregnancy issue.

I guess it all boils down to the old mortality thing. Having kids that late in life helps you keep the illusion that you're going to live forever. But nature's reality is quite different. Often at an advanced age, the male dies immediately following copulation, as evidenced by the midge fly.[4]

Maybe it's just nature's way of telling you something like: "Hey, menopausal mama. Get your head out of your yam cream and listen up. You're too old for this." But who listens? We all want to stay young and vigorous forever. It's an ego thing. I admit that I also feel this way. I don't ever want anybody thinking of me as old and decrepit. When I go at 104, I want my obituary to read, "Her chute didn't open."

Top Ten Reasons for Older Motherhood: More or Less

1. *Less* to share: The kids will never ask to borrow your clothes.
2. *More* options: You can always get out of PTA duties by posing as a grandparent.
3. *More* quality time: You can spend hours drinking your dinners through a straw together.

---

4. And Tony Randall.

4. *More* togetherness: Experience the fun of wearing matching mother-daughter diapers.

5. *More* bonding: You can try activities like Saturday afternoon walker races.

6. *Less* demands: Your kids will never ask you to baby-sit the grandchildren.

7. *Less* waiting: The good old days are now.

8. *More* creative playtime: You can amuse your child for hours by doing tricks with your dentures.

9. *Less* responsibility: You can finally afford a full-time nanny.

10. *More* loopholes: By the time you need to have that embarrassing discussion about sex, you'll be too old to remember anything about it.

CHAPTER

16

Matchmaker Moms:

Connubial Crapshoot

When it comes to their daughters, it seems like moms and dads work at cross purposes. A mom's ultimate goal is to find a suitable husband for her daughter. But a dad's obsession is with trying to keep his daughter a virgin for most of her natural life. Is this sicko behavior or what? Well, it's not only true but it's been going on since time began. Throughout the ages, men have been instrumental in inventing all kinds of torturous devices with only one purpose: to prevent girls from ever doing "the wild thing."

In medieval times, they made virgins wear a chastity belt.[1]

---

1. Still sold at Catholic churches everywhere.

Later on, some cultures employed barbaric circumcision practices on women to keep them from experiencing sexual pleasure.[2]

I am thoroughly familiar with this scenario. When I was in high school, my dad appointed himself the number one guardian of my youthful virginity. And it wasn't only my dad, either. Every priest in my Catholic church was in cahoots with him. The Catholics are well known for their strict adherence to papal dictates like "Thou shalt not have a good time." But everybody knows that girls just want to have fun. Therefore, it's no accident that the Church schedules confession on Saturday afternoons. It has been the best deterrent for Saturday night sex for centuries, short of placing a Colt .45 to your head.

When I was a teenager, women never thought of lobbying for their rights. We were so passive, we would have been first in line for Kool-Aid at Jonestown. Looking back, it's obvious to me that the only problem my dad and the priests had was that they needed to get a life. But thirty years later, my dad still hasn't changed. If I were dating today, he'd have a Lo-Jack installed in my pants.

However, when it comes to dads and their sons, it's a whole different ballgame.[3] As the mother of sons, I can tell

---

2. A condom would have accomplished the same thing.
3. With rules according to Steve Garvey.

you that the old double standard is still alive and thriving. Dads have always been and are still encouraging their sons to go out and get some tail. They even provide the family van to help them in their quest. They call it good parenting. I call it sexual discrimination. Every time a teenage boy scores, his dad is so proud he commemorates the event by carving another notch on the dashboard.

Every mom still believes in the sanctity of marriage. If her daughter is over twenty-five and not married, she automatically starts scouting for suitable candidates. The problem is, moms are clueless about which men are good catches. They are so desperate to grab any available man for their daughter, they don't discriminate at all. They will fix their daughter up with any man who's not attached to a respirator.

When a gal hits thirty and is still unmarried, her mom really takes it hard. She'll go to her daughter's apartment every day and sit shiva. She will constantly nag her daughter, finding fault with everything in her lifestyle. She's famous for leaving twenty-minute messages on her daughter's answering machine about why her life isn't working because she hasn't settled down. Yada, yada, yada. But what the moms don't get is that their behavior is not winning them any popularity contests. In fact, they have made themselves so unpopular, they are about the only people out there who get refunds on their Call Waiting.

From the minute she enters her daughter's apartment, a mom begins criticizing. She says things like, "Isn't it about time you got rid of those godawful Ikea tables and crates you call bookshelves? When are you going to get some *real* furniture?" That's when you offer her a futon to sleep on. *Futon* is the Japanese word for "unwanted guest."

The real problem is that for single, intelligent women with decent standards, it's slim pickin's out there. Most of the guys they meet all have one serious problem—they're married. It's either that or they eventually discover they're alcoholics, cross-dressers, or manic depressives.[4] Not to mention all the guys who are just plain fat from subsisting on Big Macs or are malnourished from eating their own cooking. Anyone who says all men are created equal has never been in a locker room.

Single gals get tired of playing those stupid mind games when they're dating. They feel they have to dress sexy and act dumb just to hold a man's interest. They happen to be right, too. Let's face it. The number one prerequisite for a successful date is a push-up bra. You have to have that boobs-on-a-half-shell look going on just to get a man to look at you.

Then, if a gal finds a guy she has real feelings for, the last thing she can do is tell him. Once she does, all she'll ever see of him is the skid marks he leaves at her doorstep. Nowadays, men are so afraid of commitment it's ridiculous. Rule of thumb: If you want a committed man, look in a mental hospital.

---

4. They'd be great guests on *Jerry Springer.*

But moms remain undaunted. All they ever talk about is the perfect guy they met in the supermarket or that wonderful eligible bachelor who's a friend of Aunt Millie's cousin's husband's brother. So you politely feign interest and let her live in her fantasy world. But after years of experiencing dates from hell, you have learned that a bachelor is just a guy who missed the opportunity to make some woman miserable.

Here's the pitch moms give their daughters when trying to sell them on their latest spousal candidate. However, their daughters may follow federal guidelines by responding with the "three strikes and you're out" law:

The Blue Collar Guy Your mom spotted him at the garage where she gets her car serviced. *The pitch:* his rugged good looks, his virility, and the fact that you'll be able to save thousands of dollars you're currently shelling out at Aamco. *Beep beep.*

Strike 1—Arrives dressed in a shirt with his name on it.

Strike 2—Took you to dinner and used the shrimp fork to clean underneath his finger nails.

Strike 3—Usually finds his dates at family reunions.

The Attorney Your mom ran into him while gawking at the scene of an accident. *The pitch:* He makes a lot of money, belongs to a country club, and uses impressive Latin phrases like *ipso facto.*

Strike 1—He's a lawyer who chases ambulances in his limo.

Strike 2—He's a sexually kinky perv who suffers from subpoena envy.

Strike 3—He wants you to sign a prenup before he agrees to date you.

The Sports Nut Your mom met him at a NASCAR convention. *The pitch:* He is more interested in participating in contact sports than in sex.

Strike 1—Showed up with a Cling-free fabric sheet stuck to his baseball jacket.

Strike 2—Spends a lot of time hanging around locker rooms with a rolled-up towel, slapping men on their butts.

Strike 3—Ninety percent of his vocabulary consists of the word *boo-ya.*

The Sensitive Guy Your mom met him at a Lifespring meeting. *The pitch:* loves puppy dogs and bunnies, isn't afraid to cry, and talks to angels.

Strike 1—Went through four boxes of tissues while watching the video *Old Yeller.*

Strike 2—Wants to have six kids in six years.

Strike 3—Needs a support group to go to the men's room.

The Older Man He and your mom had bunion surgery performed by the same podiatrist. *The pitch:* He's an adventurer who has climbed Mount Everest and his mortgage is paid off.

Strike 1—He looks more like Barnaby Jones than Indiana Jones.

Strike 2—Sets off alarms wherever he goes with his metal hip and pacemaker.

Strike 3—Needs a mirror under his mouth during sex to see if he's still breathing.

The Fitness Nut His name is Lars and he's your mom's personal trainer. *The pitch:* "Get a load of those biceps, abs, and gluts."

Strike 1—His biggest intellectual achievement was making it through the Montgomery Ward catalog.

Strike 2—In order to count to twenty-one, he has to get naked.

Strike 3—He has an unnatural preoccupation with Wesson oil and Speedo apparel.

The Nerd He's an actuarial at your mom's insurance company. *The pitch:* He may not be exciting, but he is stable, studious, and devoted to his mother.

Strike 1—Your mom's pitch.

Strike 2—Insists on wearing his pocket protector and slide rule when making love.

Strike 3—His crewcut is waxed so heavily, it could spear kabobs.

The Recovering Alcoholic Your mom met him at her local AA chapter. *The pitch:* a sweet guy who is good at apologizing, making amends, and begging for forgiveness.

Strike 1—Is so codependent, when he dies, someone else's life will pass in front of his eyes.

Strike 2—Needs a twelve-step program to pick out a movie.

Strike 3—Frequently gets beaten up after ordering Shirley Temples in a bar.

The Fat Guy Your mom met him at an all-you-can-eat buffet. *The pitch:* He has a winning personality, owns his own condo,[5] and is light on his feet.

Strike 1—He thinks *A Farewell to Arms* is a diet book.

Strike 2—He has written several fan letters to Richard Simmons.

Strike 3—No man is an island, but he comes pretty close.

---

5. Or more accurately, is his own condo.

Matchmaker Mom's Quiz

1. You fixed your daughter up with an older man who is quite set in his ways. The only thing about him she can change is his:

    a. sexual stamina

    b. musical taste

    c. TV habits

    d. diapers

2. The man you fixed your daughter up with claimed he had royalty in his family. But he turned out to be:

    a. a king of fast foods

    b. a drug czar

    c. a lord of Flatbush

    d. Prince Rogaine

3. According to your daughter, the only thing that would improve the quality of life of the last guy you found for her would be:

    a. mood elevators

    b. Viagra

    c. more money

    d. euthanasia

4. You found a great guy to escort your daughter to a black tie event. What would be the smartest thing for her to wear?
   a. a Richard Tyler gown
   b. a cocktail dress by Bagley Mishka
   c. anything designed by Oleg Cassini
   d. blinders

5. After you fixed your daughter up with a string of losers, she was forced to call:
   a. a dating service
   b. a counselor
   c. a singles club
   d. the suicide hot line—on speed dial

6. That older guy from your country club you fixed your daughter up with was famous for his:
   a. sixteen handicap
   b. new Porsche Boxter
   c. hefty bank account
   d. toupee with a zipper

7. On prom night, a dad makes sure his daughter remains a virgin by sitting:
    a. on the chaperon committee
    b. her down for an antisex lecture
    c. up all night waiting for her
    d. in the backseat of her date's car

8. You found your daughter this guy who claims to be an Italian opera singer named:
    a. Luciano Pavarotti
    b. Andrea Bocelli
    c. Ezio Pinza
    d. Tony Soprano

The answer to all of the above is *d* as in *date*.

    1–4 right: Keep her room furnished.

    5–8 right: You've got a guest room!

Mother of the Bride:

Master the Possibilities

From the moment a girl gets that ring on her finger, her mother's raison d'être is to plan the "perfect wedding." Most mothers seize this opportunity to fulfill the dreams they never got to by doing it for their daughters. Because they were from modest backgrounds, they take great pleasure in giving their daughters that big church wedding and hotel reception they never had.

Let's face it. Many of us moms had our receptions in VFW halls where the entertainment was Uncle Harry playing the accordion in his rumpled tuxedo. Given that ugly reality, that's why moms feel the need to create a fantasy wedding for their daughters. But the moms are the ones who end up living in it. Here are two of a mom's beliefs that call for a serious reality check:

1.   Her daughter is only going to get married once in her lifetime, so the wedding has to be spectacular.
2.   The groom's family will graciously kick in a few bucks to help finance the overblown event.

Based on these false premises, she blindly forges ahead, clipboard in hand, meticulously covering more ground than Louie Anderson. The first step is to search for the most expensive and annoying "wedding facilitator" money can buy.

This is a guy who has not only fabricated some chichi-sounding name for himself, like Szechwan, but a bogus title, too. He operates out of some artsy studio draped in *peau de soie* and bathed in peach-colored lighting. This guy is responsible for jacking up your bill with his plans for releasing two hundred flying doves in a humongous white wedding tent and installing champagne fountains all over the lawn. Every time another grandiose idea enters his artsy little brain, it'll cost you big time. He bills by the hour and performs more acts than Heidi Fleiss.

The mother of the bride believes that the wedding she throws will be a direct reflection of how well off the family is. Therefore, she has to compete with the lofty standards set by her wealthy girlfriends' memorable weddings. The wedding is a study in one-upsmanship. But no matter how hard she tries to make it a perfect day, guests always see weddings as the perfect vehicle to air their own personal grievances.

A wedding is an occasion where somebody always gets their feelings hurt about something. Your aunt Jocelyn is livid because the invitation states, "No children at the church, please." She is clueless as to why anybody wouldn't want the presence of her six screaming brats to defile this sacred event. Likewise, Uncle Al will be mad for the next decade when you reject the bawdy toast to the newlyweds[1] it took him six weeks to write.[2] Just expect several fistfights to break out among the invited guests when you offer the lethal combination of an open bar and bad karaoke music.

You also must expect to get into a major war with your husband over the wedding reception menu. He will vehemently defend his entree selection of chicken à la king with french fries at $9.99 a head. Whereas you and Szechwan will insist on the medallions du boeuf with truffle sauce at $29.99 per gilt-edged plate. Don't kid yourself. He's not about to take this one lying down. This battle could get to the point where you are serving papers on each other.

The florist is the next bone of contention. Your choice is the deluxe bridal bouquet made with exotic calla lilies, stephanotis, and gardenias. It will set you back at least $2,500,

---

1. Begins with "There once was a maid from Nantucket."
2. And six bottles of scotch.

because it's custom designed from the artists at House of Panache. Your husband will be boiling mad. He just doesn't understand why you can't go for something simpler and cheaper, like daffodils or daisies from Home Depot.

Szechwan will make sure that the hors d'ouevres are the latest in nouvelle cuisine. In fact, they'll be so chic that nobody will have ever heard of them before. The costly canapés will feature items like toasted yak flank served on phyllo pastries and shiitake mushrooms stuffed with rare cheeses from an island off of Corsica.

He will provide tuxedoed waiters in white gloves strolling about, serving these delicacies from huge silver platters trimmed with lace doilies and orchids. And just to make sure you don't have a red cent left, he insists that the Dom Pérignon be poured into crystal fluted champagne glasses.

Be prepared to handle a lot of logistical problems. With all the divorces among the family members and invited guests, the seating arrangements become a very complicated task. The mother of the bride requires months to strategically work it all out on a blackboard. In the end, she will use more chalk than Eisenhower did planning D day.

Family grudges, affairs, bad blood—*all* the dirty laundry gets aired on public clotheslines at a wedding. It might be a good idea to wrap a complimentary can of mace in white tissue paper and leave it at each place setting. But it might be a better idea to have the guests check their guns at the door.

There is one thing you must understand from the get-go, though. During the year it takes to plan this extravaganza, the groom's parents are going to be harder to find than Jimmy Hoffa's body. They will be lying low in a bunker, unwilling to return any of your calls. It would be easier to extract an impacted wisdom tooth than a monetary commitment from them.

You may be wondering where the bride is during all this planning. Remember, she may be the bride, but this is *your* wedding. So forge ahead, no matter how many tantrums she throws. After all, Mother knows best—and is not beyond throwing a pretty good tantrum of her own.

I never got to be a mother of the bride because I have two sons. But as the mother of the groom, I got to plan a small wedding for my son and his wife. It was a really unique wedding, too. Even though I couldn't afford a flake like Szechwan, our family already has more characters than Disney. Here's the background. My twenty-two-year-old son, Michael, became engaged to a beautiful Korean girl named Kyong Suk Seo, which in American is Whitney.[3] They met when they were students at Brigham Young University in Utah. They are both devout Mormons, as committed to their faith as they are to each other. So far, so good. The quirky part wasn't them, it's with the rest of us.

---

3. According to the pop-diva translation table.

I was divorced from Michael's dad and remarried to my current husband, Mark, who is Jewish. My other son, Philip, was a student at San Diego State University, where most of the college kids practiced hedonism. Philip, a devout Delta Tau man, had an innate fear of any zealous religion. So the night before his brother's wedding, he said to me: "Mom, don't stick me in the same room with Michael. He'll play those subliminal tapes and I'll wake up tomorrow morning with my eyes glazed over, professing to be a new member of the flock." Okay, got the picture here?[4]

The most unique thing about this wedding was the guest list. It was composed of more eclectic religions than you'd find at the Museum of Tolerance. We had the Mormon bride and groom and their Mormon friends from Utah, including a couple with thirteen (you read that right) kids. The Buddhist was represented by Whitney's sister, Sujeong Seo, who came from Korea. The Jews were represented by my husband, his parents, and his brother. The special category of excommunicated Catholics were proudly represented by my sister and me. The rest were heathens represented by the delegation from San Diego State. Party on, dudes.

I did not have an open bar for three reasons:

1.   It was too costly for my budget.

2.   The Jewish contingency weren't big drinkers anyway.

---

4. And out of focus.

3.   The strongest thing ever passing through a Mormon kidney is Ovaltine.

As a result, the guests were all on their best behavior and no major wars broke out between the East and West. I guess an imaginary Gaza Strip ran right through the cocktail lounge. Also, the guests were well aware that if they didn't behave, the menopausal mother of the groom[5] might crack under the strain and drown herself in the punch bowl.

I felt incredible pressure to try and successfully integrate all the different cultures popping into my life. I spent weeks memorizing the twelve tribes of Israel and the contents of the golden tablets, delivered by Joseph Smith, who acted as the divine postman.[6] Then I had to switch gears and learn how to pronounce basic Yiddish words like *machatunum* (in-laws) and *ganza macher* (big shot) with the proper ethnic accent. I also had to make sure I did it without spitting in anyone's face. If not, I'd have to look forward to a lifetime of being known as "the dumb shiksa" by the Jewish side of the family.

I ordered a wedding cake with the politically correct mixed ethnic bride and groom figurines on top. I also served ethnically correct canapés like potato knishes and kimchee. Add the mini-corndogs on a stick and the de rigueur keg for the college kids and everybody felt right at home. So I didn't

---

5. That would be me.

6. The role was subsequently given to Kevin Costner.

spend a fortune on that big, white tent, the gourmet sit-down dinner, and the ice sculpture. I offended no one. The Mylanta flowed freely. *L'Chaim*. The only one who suffered any indignity or stress was, you guessed it, *moi,* the mom.

All of this intermarrying produced quite an extended family for the bride and groom. Mark had kids from his previous marriage who became their stepsisters. His parents became their stepgrandparents, and his brother, wife, and kids became—I'll be damned if I know. Also, Whitney is from a family of ten brothers and sisters, all living in Korea. So our new extended family branched out in all directions. In fact, our family tree has more tentacles than the creature from *Alien*.

Mother of the Bride Etiquette Quiz

1. The best etiquette book for a wedding is the one written by:
   a. Emily Post
   b. Amy Vanderbilt
   c. Martha Stewart
   d. Tonya Harding

2. The only person who should not wear gloves at a wedding is:
   a. the bride
   b. the mother of the bride
   c. the flower girl
   d. O.J.

3. When is it proper to send a "regrets only" card?
   a. three weeks prior to the wedding
   b. immediately after receiving the invitation
   c. one week before the wedding
   d. right after appearing on *Who Wants to Marry a Millionaire.*

4. In a Jewish–Catholic wedding, where would you find the Jewish mother of the bride sitting?
   a. in the first row of pews
   b. in the narthex
   c. on the left side of the church
   d. shiva

5. The father of the bride feels that a lovely wedding gift would be a complete place setting for twelve of:
   a. Royal Doulton
   b. Wedgwood
   c. Limoges
   d. Chinette

6. What is the wedding videographer's favorite part to film?
   a. the communion service
   b. the reception
   c. the prenuptial dinner
   d. the postcoital cigarette

7. In a divorced family, where is the best place to seat your ex-husband and his new wife?
   a. anywhere on the left side of the church
   b. front pew, left side of the church
   c. second row, right side of the church
   d. in the basement

8. Beside the groom, who else wears tuxedos?
   a. members of the wedding party
   b. members of the catering staff
   c. members of the immediate family
   d. members of the crime family

9. Which prenuptial parties should not be video-graphed?
   a. the bridal shower
   b. the prenuptial dinner
   c. the engagement party
   d. the stag party

10. In which part of the wedding will you always catch the father of the bride crying?
    a. the exchange of wedding vows
    b. when his daughter says, "I do"
    c. giving his daughter away at the altar
    d. giving his check away to the caterers

The answer to all of the above is *d* as in *I don't*.

10–7 right Excellent. A bouquet of roses to you!

6–4 right: Fair. Have a bottle of Asti Spumante.

3–0 right: Booby prize. You get your kid's new in-laws for the weekend.

Retired Moms:

The Dulcolax Decade

Dad has been retired for a number of years, but Mom hasn't been able to. She's still employed in the full-time job of baby-sitting him. To put it mildly, he's a handful. They retired to a small town in Florida called Sandalfoot, where the fun never starts. My mom describes her life as being very "full"— "uneventful" and "unremarkable." Her day begins at 4:30 A.M. and ends at 6:30 P.M. No wonder she's bored. Hellooooo. What on earth is there to do between the hours of 4:30 and 9:00 A.M.? The whole world is in a coma during those hours.

My day begins around 9:30 A.M. and ends at midnight. Because there is a whopping three-hour time difference between coasts, Mom's schedule makes it really tough for us to phone each other. With those insane 4:30 to 6:30 hours, we're only able to talk during a five-minute window of opportunity when we're both awake.

Grateful to be alive at eighty-five, Mom waxes sentimental about growing old with platitudes like: "Screw the golden years." Okay, so now you've got an idea of what Mom's all about. Party hearty. This is the thing about older women. By the age of seventy, they all turn into Sophia from *The Golden Girls*. Whatever thought pops into their heads is out of their mouths before you can say the word *censorship*. If I tell her that my son has a new girlfriend, she says, "Just pray he doesn't knock her up." Gee, thanks, Mom. Don't sugarcoat it—give it to me straight. My mom explains it this way: "At my age, if I can't say it, it backs up and comes out some other place."

Most retired women spend the greater part of their existence complaining about their husbands being underfoot. The worst moment in their lives was the day their husbands came home and announced, "Honey, I'm home—*for good!*" Retired women all say the same thing: Their husbands need to get "a life." It's very common for retired men to start living their wives' lives. Mom says every time she starts to leave the house to go shopping, Dad turns into Torquemada and holds an Inquisition:

"Where are you going?"

"How long will you be gone?"

"What about my lunch?"

"Do you really need to go right now?"

"Why can't I come with you?"

Geez, Louise. Haven't women already gone through this with their kids? It's like being Mommy all over again. Will there ever be a time in our lives when women don't have to answer to somebody? Oh, sure. When Donald Trump tweezes his eyebrows.

When Mom is on the phone, Dad is right there in her face, asking her stupid stuff every two seconds. She says it's worse than having a three-year-old pestering her all day. Every call becomes a three-way conversation. When I am trying to talk with her on the phone, she has to interrupt our conversation a million times to answer Dad. It's a hundred times more annoying than Call Waiting, trust me. Here's a typical ménage à trois à la phone:

> MOM TO ME: Just a minute, Jan.
>
> MOM TO DAD: Hold your horses, Frank. Let me finish my conversation with Jan.
>
> MOM TO ME: Okay, Jan. You were saying . . . ugh . . . just a sec. . . .
>
> MOM TO DAD: Yes, she's back from her trip. . . . I don't know . . . so let me ask her. . . .
>
> MOM TO ME: Your father wants to know if you're planning on visiting us before the next millennium.

ME TO MOM: Tell him to chill out.

MOM TO DAD: Frank, your daughter says to chill out. Ha ha.

MOM TO ME: Now I forgot what I wanted to ask you . . . *(sotto voce)* He's driving me nuts. . . . I have to repeat everything ten times to him.

ME TO MOM: Maybe he's getting hard of hearing. Do you think he needs a hearing aid?

MOM TO ME: He doesn't need a hearing aid, he just needs a haircut.

MOM TO DAD: Well, I thought it was funny. . . .

At this point, I know she's contemplating adding roach killer to his Ensure. It's either that or strangulation with the phone cord.

When women get to be the age of seventy-five, it seems like every few weeks one of their friends passes away. And usually, it's one of their girlfriends' husbands. My mom has lived in Florida for the past fifteen years, and her next-door neighbor has already buried three husbands.[1]

When widows get together for cards, they always talk about their dead husbands. There are lots of stories about what Harry or Johnny did when he was alive. The conversations are frequently peppered with the phrase "May he rest in peace." But from the way they're raking those poor dead

---

1. And two of them were just napping.

guys over the coals, it would be more accurate if they said, "May he rest in peace—until I get there."

There are several things you need to know when visiting your retired parents. For openers, they have way too much time on their hands. This makes them arrive one to two hours early every place they go. Their cocktail hour is at three P.M. Dinner is at 4:30. Bedtime at nine P.M., like clockwork. Retired parents are less flexible than Charlton Heston on gun control. So when they tell you to come for dinner at five P.M., *do not be late.* By 5:10, they're pacing. By 5:20, they're on the phone, yelling, "Where the hell are you?" By 5:25, they've got steam coming out of their ears. If you dare show up at their door anytime after that, you'd better come armed.

Another thing about retired moms (and dads) is that they are totally oblivious to the technological revolution the world is undergoing. They are still the only group on the planet who refuse to get an answering machine. Even the chimpanzees in Sumatra have them installed in their trees. But Mom and Dad? Forget it. Mom says, "What do I need one of those things for? I'm home all the time anyway."[2]

The truth of the matter is that all those new electronic gadgets are just too intimidating for them. There are twenty years' worth of videos stockpiled in their closets because they

---

2. A direct shot at my dad, but his ear hair prevents him from hearing it.

have never learned how to operate the VCR I gave them. It's just another item that is supposed to make their lives easier, but ends up making it harder. Every time they try to figure out how to use it, they start bickering and calling each other "moron." Ditto for everything else in the house that comes with a manual. It's like they are being held captive by their appliances.

I kid my mom about this all the time. I tell her to wake up and join the twenty-first century. If she just got a computer, we could E-mail each other like the rest of the family does. But even the mention of the word *computer* freaks her out. For God's sake, even my iron has a computer chip that tells me I have E-mail. However, I instinctively know that if I ever showed her my Palm Pilot V, she'd have a coronary.

My folks are also among the handful of *Homo sapiens* who do not have central air-conditioning. They still have window units. And even then, they only turn them on when the temperature gets above ninety-five degrees and algae begins growing on their walls.

It isn't a money issue, either. It's about total resistance to change. My folks' house has the original plumbing and electrical systems that were installed by Thomas Edison. And God forbid, something goes on the fritz.[3] Both my parents go into a panic worse than Orson Welles created with his *War of the Worlds* radio broadcast.

---

3. An archaic term only used by people over seventy-five.

Old age comes at a bad time, that's for sure. Mom complains that Dad has no energy. She says he takes a nap immediately after he wakes up. Then they turn on the TV and watch the soaps all afternoon. Another tip when you're visiting your parents: Don't mess with their programming. Old people tell time by what TV shows are on. Their evening lineup starts with *Wheel of Fortune* and ends with *Who Wants to Be a Millionaire.* If anybody changed the channels, they'd become so disoriented, they would be eating their pot roast with Katie Couric at seven A.M.

Retired moms' calendars are filled with their doctor appointments. Arthritis, circulatory problems, and cataracts are an integral part of dealing with the struggles of advanced age. My mom has reached the point where she is so immersed in her own health miseries, she has little patience for any of my problems. One day when I was complaining to her about something that happened to me as "the worst feeling in the world," she shot back: "Worst feeling in the world? Try going without a bowel movement for ten days."[4]

Even though she is physically ailing, Mom's mind is still as sharp as a tack. Recently she had a vision problem and, fearing it might be a stroke, Dad took her to the emergency room. As she was being examined, the doctors and nurses barraged her with questions to see if her faculties were still

---

4. Another Metamucil moment.

intact. They asked her age, what day it was, what year it was, her kids' names, and so on. She ran out of patience real fast with these questions she considered just plain stupid. So when they got to "Who is the president of the United States?" she replied, "Who the hell do you think? Everybody knows it's Hillary."

They were not amused. I thought it was priceless. Way to go, Mom!

Are You Ready for Retirement?

Choose: Always (A), Sometimes (S), or Never (N)

1. Does the expression "pull the plug" frequently come up in your everyday conversations? (A) (S) (N)

2. Would you ever patronize a restaurant that doesn't offer a "two-fer" coupon? (A) (S) (N)

3. Are you considering the possibility of replacing all your eating utensils with straws? (A) (S) (N)

4. Is your osteoporosis so bad, you're wearing your panty hose as a tube top? (A) (S) (N)

5. Does your husband sneak into the kitchen after you're asleep to rescrub the pots and pans? (A) (S) (N)

6. Nowadays, are all your phone calls completed by six A.M.? (A) (S) (N)

7. Does your answering machine message consist solely of you repeating things like: "Is this on?" "How do I get this to work?" "Where's the damn button?" (A) (S) (N)

8. Do the words *assisted care living* produce chills up your spine? (A) (S) (N)

9. Do you feel you're at a place where you have no issues with blue hair rinse? (A) (S) (N)

10. Do you insist on keeping the thermostat at eighty-five degrees year-round? (A) (S) (N)

If you answered more than six with *A*, start using your early-bird coupons and wearing your sandals with socks.

Grand Moms:

Do It to Me One More Time

There are so many wonderful things about being a grandma, I'd be hard pressed to name all of them. But from my unique perspective, let me tell you about the items I'd put in the asset column. The truth is that being a grandma combines the best of all worlds. You get to have a baby with none of the responsibility or physical work. Isn't that a neat trick? Even though I loved raising my kids, there's no way I'd want to be a mother all over again. Why? Here are just a few of the items that go on the debit side of the page:

Morning Sickness

If ever a name was a misnomer, this is it. Ask any woman[1] who was ever pregnant, and she'll tell you that morning sickness lasts twenty-four hours a day for at least three months. And this is if you're lucky. Some women spend the whole nine months hugging the porcelain Honda. Even if you're not tossing your cookies, you live in a perpetual state of queasiness. I remember that any kind of smell, from popcorn to salmon, made me gag. Then when I actually ate something, I'd really pay the price. Talk about sick. Mariah Carey and her oysters had nothing on me.

Pregnancy

Ugh. Just the word makes my ovaries go into spasm. All I remember is feeling like a beached whale for nine months. I was retaining more water than the Hoover Dam. Let me put it this way. During pregnancy, your body goes through more changes than Keanu Reeves in *The Matrix*. Your boobs swell up to the point where you can't take off your bra without sustaining a whiplash. You get these hormonal zits that erupt with greater force than Mount St. Helens. You sprout

---

1. And Arnold Schwarzenegger.

fuzz in strange places—like on your belly and upper lip. Your legs develop varicose veins the size of ziti. Whoever said that women are at their most beautiful when pregnant should be declared legally blind.

Labor and Delivery

This is another one of those experiences that is called "beautiful" by people who haven't got a clue. Well, I have. I've been there, done that—twice. And if I had to do it all over again, I'd kill myself. Either that or let Tony Soprano whack me. If I remember correctly, I was given three choices of how I was going to have the baby:

1. natural delivery
2. cesarean
3. Heimlich

My labor was the worst. It seemed like it would never end. I was in labor for about 107 days. The baby just wasn't ready to make an appearance. My ob tried everything short of coaxing him out with a pork chop. As a last resort, he tried using the Heimlich maneuver. One good squeeze and it worked like a charm. All the labor nurses breathed a sigh of relief as my son flew across the room.

I'll tell you one thing about the grandmas of today. We are totally different from the grandmas I remember. Two words:

Naomi Judd. Wow! I would have volunteered to be a grandma thirty years ago if it meant looking like her. But my grandmother was your typical old-fashioned grandma. She was a four-foot ten-inch munchkin with white hair piled on top of her head. She always wore a hair net, too. In those days, this hairdo was known as the "upsweep." We called my grandmother "Nonny" and we loved her with a passion. She was the essence of unconditional love and patience.

My sister and I spent many weekends at her home in East Haven, Connecticut. We got so used to her pampering us, our parents had to drag us back home, kicking and screaming, on Sunday nights. Besides her world-class lemon meringue pie, her Sunday-morning breakfasts were legendary. She would make us hot griddle cakes with maple syrup, porridge loaded with sugar and butter, and piles of crispy bacon. Even at the age of ten, one of these breakfasts was enough to send you to cardiac ICU for the rest of the week. But it was worth it. Grandmas never heard of cholesterol, high-density lipids, or anything else of the kind. All they knew was that if they didn't add a pound of butter and a can of Crisco to whatever they baked, it tasted like crap.

In comparison, I'm a grandma who has gotten totally sucked into the health food thing. My regular hangouts are Whole Foods and Jamba Juice. I go into Jamba every day, without fail, for my carrot and wheat-grass juice. The minute I walk in the door, all the kids who work there call out, "Hi,

Jan." It's great. I feel just like Norm on *Cheers*.[2] But it makes me sad to think that my granddaughter is never going to get to taste Nonny's world-class pies or cakes. All she's ever going to get out of my kitchen is a rice cake with a wheat-grass shooter. Gag me with a spoon.

Today's grandmas look vastly different in appearance from the grandmas of my day. Remember when everyone's grandma had either blue- or lilac-tinted hair? They also always had some half-dead corsage pinned on their dresses. And during Christmas, fuggeddaboudit. They had the entire Nativity scene plastered across their bosoms. But nowadays, grandmas are no longer the gray-haired, kindly-looking old women who wear polka-dotted silk dresses and pearls around their necks. Oh oh. Wait a second. Somebody had better book Barbara Bush on *Jenny Jones* for a makeover.

The grandmas of today are more likely to wear tight capri pants and clingy sweaters. That can only mean one thing—a lot of lard being packed under perilous pressure in our twenty-four-hour bras and girdles. God help any bystander if we suffer a spontaneous blowout. We're talking cellulite traveling at warp speed. Prepare for impact, Sulu. Hey, I never said we grandmas look great in these outfits, I just said we wear them.

I remember both my grandmas wearing garters to hold up their stockings. They were round elastics that they rolled

---

2. "You want to be where everyone knows your name."

the tops of their hose over, pulled up to just above the knee. And when they sat down with their knees apart,[3] trust me, it wasn't pretty. They looked like they were wearing condoms on their legs. Today's grandmas wouldn't be caught dead wearing those things. The only kind of garters grandmas wear nowadays are the kind attached to a lacy belt—from Victoria's Secret.

In our age-conscious society, a lot of grandmas are reluctant to admit they are grandmas. They're still trying to pass themselves off as their kids' older sisters on the days they're taking diuretics. Sometimes we go as far as discouraging the baby from calling us "Grandma." I know a lot of women who make their grandkids call them "sweetie," "honey," or even by their first names. But that's not my thing. My granddaughter can call me anything she wants—Grammy, Nana, or Grandma. Anything except—"Mee-Maw." Where on earth did that one come from anyway? I'll tell you one thing. If my granddaughter ever starts calling me "Mee-Maw," I'd have no choice but to lace her Enfamil with ipecac.

One thing that will never change about grandmas is that we feel compelled to show pictures of our grandchildren to everyone we come across, including total strangers. We have albums filled with an entire pictorial history of our grandchildren from the time they were fetuses until their wedding days. We should own stock in the Kodak company. I will

---

3. The classic grandma way of sitting.

admit to conditioning my granddaughter like one of Pavlov's dogs. The minute I say, "Sarah, look at Grandma," she stops what she's doing and poses for me with her great, big smile. It's a grandma's S.O.P. never to walk out the door without a camera hanging from her neck. I guess we all live with the same delusion—we're going to be the next Anne Geddes.

We have appointed ourselves as the family historian, recording all of the baby's "firsts." First step. First smile. First poop. All these events are of equal importance in a grandma's eyes.

And, of course, grandmas set the standards for bias. When I describe how exquisitely beautiful Sarah is to anyone who will listen, I put it this way: "She makes Catherine Zeta-Jones look like Bea Arthur."

I look at being a grandma as payback time. A grandkid gives you a second chance to make up for all the sins of omission you committed when you were a parent. Like all the times you were on the phone, working late, or just too tired to play with your kid. We have carried that guilt around for way too long. So now we have a chance to redeem those frequent-flyer miles for all the guilt trips.

Where I was stricter than a general with my own kids,[4] I'm putty in Sarah's hands. When she says, "Gamma, I love you," it's over. She could get away with anything short of burning down

---

4. My kids had to pull their own diaper duty.

the house. My sons are bowled over by this sappy side of me they've never seen. But for me, it's simple. I have one mission: to spoil them rotten, then leave the premises.

And when she says, "Gamma, play with me," I will color or read with her, sitting cross-legged on the floor for hours, until my legs are numb. Then I'll jump up[5] and play peek-a-boo or hide-and-go-seek for as long as she wants. Hey, I'm in no hurry. I've got a lifetime of karma to work out.

Grandmas R Us Quiz

1. As a young mom, you lived in your Levi 501s. Now that you're a grandmother, you can only fit into:
    a. Dockers
    b. sweatpants
    c. Gap khakis
    d. Levi 1002s

2. What is the one thing you miss most about your pregnancy?
    a. feeling the baby kick
    b. hearing the baby's heartbeat
    c. the miracle of birth
    d. those pants with the expanding tummy

---

5. And immediately fall down from lack of circulation.

3. What one practice is still the same in the hospital labor rooms?
    a. choice of anesthesia
    b. mirror to watch the birth
    c. the soothing music
    d. the complimentary enema

4. The only downside to being a grandmother is now you have to:
    a. change diapers again
    b. baby-sit for free
    c. worry when they get sick
    d. sleep with a grandfather

5. When you had your baby, you left the hospital with which memento:
    a. a portrait of your newborn
    b. complimentary hat and booties
    c. a case of disposable diapers
    d. a case of hemorrhoids

6. As a doting grandma, you think nothing of paying $5,000 for:
   a. your grandkid's medical bills
   b. preschool tuition
   c. a family vacation to Disneyland
   d. the last Tickle-Me Elmo at Toys "R" Us

7. Hospitals are not using forceps anymore to help the baby get through the birth canal in difficult deliveries. Instead, they're using:
   a. birthing chairs
   b. suction machines
   c. the Le Boyer baths
   d. bungee cords

8. What kind of shot do grandmas most frequently recommend for babies with colic?
   a. vitamin B_{12}
   b. folic acid
   c. vitamin E
   d. Jack Daniels

The answer to all of the above is *d* as in *doting*.
1–4 right: Better dye your hair blue.
5–8 right: Go, Granny!

CHAPTER
20

Millennium Moms:

The Cyberhouse Rules

When you look at the whole mom thing from a historical perspective, you've got to wonder if moms have changed that much over the years. I think we'd all like to believe that we haven't. We still want to keep that image of June Cleaver, handing out chocolate-chip cookies and Kool-Aid to the neighborhood kids. But the truth is that because our society is evolving at such a frantic pace, moms have to change to keep up with it. In today's psychotic existence, moms are more like June Cleaver on mescaline.

When I was a young mom, I thought I was really doing great just getting my butt out of bed every morning at 6:30 A.M. to get the kids up for school. Then, if I actually got their lunches made, I'd award myself the Good Housekeeping Seal of Approval. That's me, the queen of low expectations. But today, moms need a live-in time-management specialist just to make it through the day. Today's young moms not only have to cover the whole school thing, but many of them have big-time careers going as well. All the added responsibility has made motherhood a whole lot harder. Let's take an overview of the crucial stages in our lifetime careers as moms:

Conception

In the past fifteen years, this aspect of motherhood has gone through the most dramatic changes of all. Nowadays, the technology available to help women conceive is like out of *Star Trek*. The simple fact is that pregnancy hardly requires a man anymore.[1] You've got your in-vitro fertilization, your gametophyte intra-fallopian transfer, your cloning, or whatever else the test tube can conceive. Pun intended. In the millennium, men have some bad news to face. They are rapidly becoming obsolete. As a species, their usefulness on the planet has been relegated to:

1. sperm donation
2. lawn maintenance

---

1. Spock or Data available upon request.

• • •

But, hey, somebody's got to do it. The good news is that neither of these functions comes cheap. The going rate for a batch of sperm for artificial insemination is about a hundred dollars. Is this outrageous or what? When I was in college, the stuff was free. In fact, there was so much of it around the place, we were, like, tripping over it.

The ironic thing is that most women spend the first half of their lives trying *not* to get pregnant. Then during the second half, it's all we can think about. Conception becomes a career goal. Most women spend the best years of their lives at some fertility clinic, voluntarily lying on a slant board with their legs up in the air. Talk about obsessive. I'll tell you one thing. I wouldn't have been caught dead doing this. Not even in the most posh surroundings—like the genuine leather backseat of a Cadillac De Ville.

My mom scoffs at all this hoopla and refers to the Gen X's as "loopy." Women of her generation just can't understand the lengths that women of today's generation are willing to go through with their test tubes and high-tech apparatus. Mom says: "I don't see why you gals can't get pregnant the old-fashioned way like I did—with a bottle of gin."

Nowadays, conception is big business. But the bad news is that all the sex (i.e., the fun) has been taken out of it. It's all about test tubes, thermometers, hormone shots, and ovulation charts. About as exciting as doing a new program by

Microsoft.[2] I don't know about you, but the thought of having to test my cervical mucus every month is enough to keep me childless forever. You're also never going to find me douching with vinegar to increase my chances of having a girl or using some kind of oil to produce a boy. Forget it. I'd rather make a salad. I'm telling you flat out. I'd never go through any of these technological nightmares. About the only high-tech method I'd agree to is conceiving on the Internet and having it delivered by FedEx next day.

Infancy

The most striking thing about today's moms is that they spend 99 percent of their time breast-feeding their babies. That's a lot of moo juice, baby. Is it any wonder that we're watching Mike Wallace interviewing a crop of ninety-pound two-year-olds? When my daughter-in-law had a baby last year, I got a whole new education on breast-feeding. In my opinion, this whole breast-feeding thing has gotten way out of control. It's become a cult thing. I mean, these women are totally brainwashed into it. It's breast-feed, breast-feed, breast-feed. And God forbid you give your baby an occasional bottle. They'll have you believing he will grow up to be Charles Manson.

The indoctrination process starts the second you con-

---

2. Or doing Bill Gates.

ceive. Even before you finish your last puff of that postcoital cigarette, the La Leche League starts banging on your door. Then three and a half minutes after you deliver, they send a lactation consultant, a.k.a. breast policeman, into your room. As I see it, this is a person who's sole purpose in life is to browbeat you into tears. The lactation consultants also follow you home to harass you even further. They want to make sure you don't dare slip the kid a bottle in a weak moment—like after being up eighty-six straight hours with a screaming newborn and on the verge of suicide.

But their worst fear is that if your baby takes a bottle, he's doomed to experience "nipple confusion." This is their term for a heinous condition that supposedly messes up your kid's ability to distinguish a bottle nipple from the real thing. Duh. How lame is that? I guess they think that the kid may reach adulthood and mistakenly make love to an Evenflo.

When a lactating mom gets sent home from the hospital,[3] her life will revolve around a mechanical device called the breast pump. The latest models are electrical, similar to the milking machines they hook up to cows on Wisconsin dairy farms. This torturous device enables you to pump breast milk efficiently, so you can refrigerate it for future use.[4] I really have an innate fear of these things. I'm not so sure that these

---

3. Thirty minutes after delivering.
4. Like when your kid is in college.

machines aren't sucking your brains out along with all that milk. Your life becomes an endless supply of nursing pads, nursing bras, cracked nipples, and counting cc's of expressed breast milk. Ugh! Is it any wonder that penis envy has made such a resurgence in the Gen X women?

Playtime

It's amazing how much playgrounds have changed since I was a kid. They no longer build anything that's pointed, sharp, or any fun to mess around with. At the risk of sounding like my great-grandfather, I'll relate this story anyway. In my day, a playground made a man out of you. It was like going to survival camp in the middle of the Amazonian jungle. But we're talking asphalt jungle here. First of all, they had these eight-foot-high monkey bars anchored in solid concrete. There was no safety net to catch you if you fell. If you took a header off of one of these things, when you woke up, your clothes would be out of style.

Then they had those thirty-foot-high metal slides with the slippery rungs you attempted to climb in your patent leather Mary Janes. The chances of making it up to the top without slipping and fracturing your jaw were slim to none. Once you got to the top, you sat down bare-legged on metal that was exposed to the blazing sun and hotter than a Bessamer furnace. By the time you got to the bottom, you needed skin grafts.

Ditto for the wooden seesaws, erected around the same time that women got the vote. They were basically telephone poles pitched over a metal fulcrum. After a fifteen-minute cheesy ride, you spent the rest of the day picking splinters out of your butt and legs. And when some fat kid the size of Moby Dick got on the other end, you knew you were in deep trouble. The second his butt made contact with the seat, you were catapulted right into traffic.

Discipline

I'm not ashamed to say that when I was raising my kids, I ran a pretty tight ship around my house. However, it occasionally sprang a leak. Basically, I yelled and screamed about the same things that my mother did. Not so today. Kids nowadays are never "troublemakers"—they have "issues." Get real. When my kids acted like monsters, I wasn't afraid to give them a spanking. You got a problem with that?

But nowadays, that same spanking could land you in family court. So be afraid. Be very afraid. The bad news is that many "progressive parents" have unwittingly handed over the reins of control to their kids. No wonder spanking has become obsolete. It's been replaced by the totally ineffectual practice of calling a "time-out." I'd like somebody to tell me how this lameo-yuppie practice ever got popular. Does anyone actually believe that it works?

Let's see—it goes something like this: Your kids get totally obnoxious and start smacking each other in the face. So you call a "time-out" and send them to their fully equipped state-of-the-art bedrooms. There, under house arrest, their punishment is to fool around on the 'Net, getting into forbidden sex chat rooms or playing violent video games until dinner. Go figure.

This generation of moms still hears their mothers' voices in their heads reciting the same old set of rules, over and over. So in turn, they recite them to their kids. The only difference is that the changing times have dictated some modifications:

THEN: Don't run with scissors in your hand. You might fall and put your eye out.

NOW: Don't run with a cell phone in your hand. You could fall and damage the microchip.

THEN: Finish your glass of milk. It builds strong bones.

NOW: Finish your low-fat mocha frappaccino latte. It costs the same as your Rollerblades.

THEN: If you don't shape up, I'm sending you to boarding school.

NOW: If you don't shape up, you're going into rehab.

THEN: Take that gum out of your mouth.

NOW: Take that stud out of your tongue.

THEN: Don't talk back to your teachers.

NOW: Don't say a word unless counsel is present.

Family Life

In my mother's day, the philosophy was "never spare your kids from anything." But in today's society, parents go to extremes to shelter their kids from everything. Like any normal married couple, my folks had their share of fights. And when they got mad at each other, they just let it all hang out in front of us. In a way, it was really good because we saw what married life was really all about. Not like the politically correct, sugar-coated stuff going on in homes today. This is why these kids can't cope with anything. They are in therapy, their parents are in therapy, and even the family dog is in therapy. So what's happening here? Why can't kids handle anything anymore? I'll tell you why. Whenever anything bad happens,[5] the prevailing mindset is "Wait until the kids are sixty before we tell them."

In my family, we saw it all. Let's get real here. Every family has their share of weirdos and loopy characters. My family made the characters in a John Waters movie look normal by comparison. What family doesn't have an Uncle Bob who shouldn't be left alone with the kiddies, or an Aunt Marge who gets plastered at all the family get-togethers?

---

5. To good people, of course.

Here's my unsolicited advice: Don't hide these folks in the closet along with your other family skeletons. Let 'em parade around for everyone to see. Where else are you going to get this kind of entertainment for free?

Historical Moms' Famous Last Words

GANDHI'S MOM: "Eat something. You're skin and bones."

BEN FRANKLIN'S MOM: "Get inside and quit playing with that cockamamie kite!"

O.J.'S MOM: "When are you going to get rid of those dirty old gloves?"

BOB PACKWOOD'S MOM: "Keep your hands to yourself."

NERO'S MOM: "Stop fiddling around with those matches!"

DR. JEKYLL/MR. HYDE'S MOM: "What's wrong? You don't seem like yourself today."

DAVID COPPERFIELD'S MOM: "You're getting on my nerves. Why don't you just disappear for a while?"

ALEXANDER GRAHAM BELL'S MOM: "What's with you? Are you so busy you can't pick up the phone once in a while?"

TONY SOPRANO'S MOM: "Why can't you refuse the offer?"

EINSTEIN'S MOM: "What's with all the graphs and symbols? Can't you write like a regular person?"

MICHAEL JACKSON'S MOM: "Don't be such a stranger. I hardly recognize you anymore."

OSCAR DE LA HOYA'S MOM: "You'll never amount to anything if you don't quit your damn fighting."

NAPOLEON BONAPARTE'S MOM: "For the last time— get your hands out of your pockets!"

About the Author

G. Wolfgang Selbrede

JAN KING IS THE NATIONAL best-selling author of the hysterical book *Hormones from Hell*. Her hilarious insights on women also appear in her books *It's a Girl Thing, Husbands from Hell, Hormones from Hell II, PMS Crazed, Male Bashing,* and *Why Men Are Clueless.*

Jan is also the author of a humor series about aging that includes *It's Better to Be Over the Hill Than Under It,* and she has written two self-help books.

Jan was a biology teacher in an inner-city high school before she began her writing career in the 1980s with a humor column in *Women's Image* magazine.

She has been a frequent guest on national daytime TV talk shows, including *Jenny Jones, Montel, Ricki Lake, Leeza,* and the *Today* show, where she roasted Matt Lauer on his fortieth birthday with her book *40 Deal with It.*

Jan is married to publisher Mark Chutick and is the mother of two sons. She can be reached via her Web site: www.jankingauthor.com.